SQUEEZE LIFE

your guide to the best bare body at any age

KARLIIN BROOKS

Foreword by Russell Simmons

Skyhorse Publishing

Skyhorse Publishing books may be
purchased in bulk at special discounts
for sales promotion, corporate gifts,
fund-raising, or educational purposes.
Special editions can also be created to
specifications. For details, contact the
Special Sales Department, Skyhorse
Publishing, 307 West 36th Street, 11th Floor,
New York, NY 10018 or
info@skyhorsepublishing.com.

Skyhorse® and Skyhorse Publishing®
are registered trademarks of Skyhorse
Publishing, Inc.®, a Delaware corporation.

Visit our website at
www.skyhorsepublishing.com.

10 9 8 7 6 5 4 3 2 1

Library of Congress Cataloging-in-
Publication Data is available on file.

Cover design by Laura Klynstra
Cover photo by SALT
ISBN: 978-1-5107-2502-7
Ebook ISBN: 978-1-5107-2503-4

Printed in China

PHOTOGRAPHERS
Layla Love
PJ Spaniol III (Cover)
Vienna Rye
Demetrius Fordham
Aja
Kermit Mercado
Ashja Moore
Brooke Fleming
Julia Corbett
Jason Nastaszewski

MODELS
Sarina Kalmogo
Kimberly Brooks
Lucy Ageeva
Cameron McCartney
Brooke Fleming
Samantha
Erin Schrode
Aesha Waks
Rebecca Schecter
Devan Dubois
Lily Brodsky
Sabine
Adam Aye
Alexis Germaine
Camilla Noelle
Samantha Lubrano
Tai Walker
Nathaniel Sol

PRODUCERS
Rebecca H James
Paul Wharton

CLEANSE AUTHOR (editor)
Katherine Krauss

PRODUCTION CREW
Trevis Wimer

Dane Wimer

GRAPHIC ARTISTS
Peter Blossom
Marko Radojevic
Matt Occhuizzo
Hillary Ramos
Nicole Richards
Brian Holder

PROJECT MANAGER
Vienna Rye

ASSISTANT PROJECT
MANAGER
Katherine Browne
Brooke Fleming

ART DIRECTION
Vienna Rye
Peter Blossom
Layla Love
Jonathan Irons

WARDROBE
Pia Malatesta
Marrya

HAIR
Jose Lopez
Jezz Hill

MAKEUP
Deshawn Hatcher
Lauren Caputi
Jezz Hill

FOOD STYLISTS
Frenchie
Jonathan Irons
Rebecca Schechter

To my loving parents, who thought I would practically die of malnutrition as a vegan teenager. Look, I made it! Alive and healthy.

To Scruffy, my very first four-legged companion, who taught me compassion for ALL creatures.

To my dear friend, detox guru Gil Jacobs who taught me everything I know about outstanding cellular health.

CONTENTS

#THIRSTY

#HUNGR

WHY THIS BOOK IS IMPORTANT TO ME

I was a normal American broad who grew up eating what everyone around me was eating. I loved Ding Dongs, pizza, pig lips and assholes, affectionately known as hot dogs; I was into anything that came from a box or an industrial deep fryer and devoured it down with gusto.

I saw a PETA video on factory farming my sophmore year of high school. I bawled my eyes out, and I thought, *I'm going to die if I don't do something to help these animals*. I became vegan overnight and started the first animal rights club in my high school. It occurred to me that humans very much

love animals and don't want them to suffer, but they also don't want to sit there and read about their suffering, their pain, and how human involvement is contributing to that.

I did not know how to approach people in a way that would inspire them to throw down for animals, for their own temples, and for the planet at large, so that they would willingly sacrifice animal products from their diets.

For twelve years I worked in TV production, whooping it up in NYC and turning my loft into a no-kill shelter. Having a complete inability to turn my back on a four-legged friend in need, I amassed a gaggle of animals that could have had gotten me cuffed and stuffed by the Department of Health and Mental Hygiene. All this, after a recent move from an apartment from which I was evicted due to "harboring homeless animals" in violation of my three-animal-max lease. I had also recently divorced my partner of nine years.

During this period of career-building and armchair activism (a very, very hands-off way of contributing to the cause of animals rights) the one thing I overlooked was my health—being a stress case and a junk food vegan wreaked havoc on the ol' mind, body, and spirit.

What eventually got me hooked somewhat obsessively on health was a battle against osteoporosis, Grave's disease, and amenorrhea, the result of a decade of total psychic and physical neglect. This was my mega call to action and hence my journey to radiant health commenced.

I decided I had to get out of the bleachers and play full tilt boogie. Standing around a friend's kitchen island during one of the "21-day vegan challenges" I had launched in NYC, a few like-minded vegan dames and I came up with the Squeeze concept. I dumped my production locations company, my boyfriend, and that little nay-saying voice in my head on auto spin, and built New York's first raw vegan food truck. It was high

time I began to put the kind raw food detox lifestyle on blast in an effort to "mobilize" people to take care of themselves and the planet by way of a rolling ready juice truck.

I have been a catalyst for many people's health journeys. There are few things that you can do to impact a person's life more powerfully, profoundly, and permanently than changing their diet. I attribute everything good in my life to this raw foods dietary shift. Every smidgen of food you eat has a direct impact on your body, mind, and spirit.

I feel younger, happier, healthier, more vibrant, hotter, and more bad-assy than I did in my teens.

It's taken a shit ton of work to reclaim my great health and my bliss, but I wake up every morning feeling energized, upbeat, and healthy. Pleasure and health go hand in hand—You can't have one without the other, like Sinatra in '58. My autoimmune disease—Grave's—is gone. Osteoporosis— gone. If doctors advocated for a raw diet and recommended it to patients there would be virtually no degenerative illnesses.

So c'mon, let's get to elevating your nutrition, kitchen, and ethics game. I need to arm you with a bunch of info so that you can kick a bunch of ass on your own and be the baddest motherfucker in the kitchen. I got your back. Veggies got your back. Let's stretch you beyond your comfort zone.

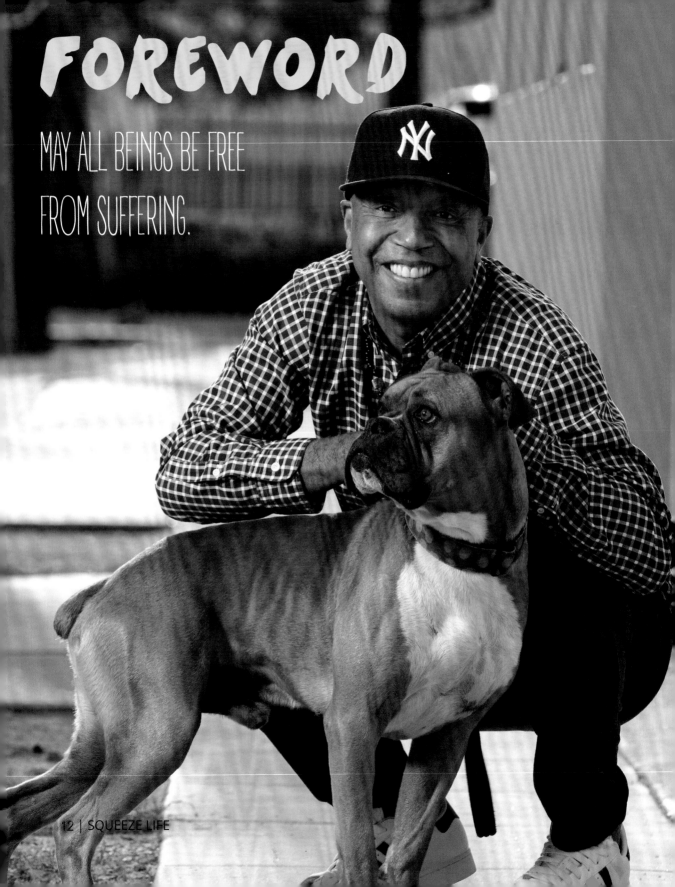

FOREWORD

MAY ALL BEINGS BE FREE FROM SUFFERING.

I do my best to live my life according to that mantra, which is why I'm a mindful eater. I practice mindful eating by being a thoughtful vegan, which I have been for over a decade. I can honestly say that what you put into your body greatly impacts all aspects of your life. Not only are there incredible health benefits, but the peace and joy you feel from no longer contributing to so much suffering is remarkable. I'm constantly striving to improve myself by practicing yoga, by finding time for meditation, and by keeping myself focused on the things that truly matter—so, to me, it only makes sense to bring that balance into my diet. I don't want to eat foods that will decrease my quality of life, or that will cause suffering to others—and that includes animals, as well as people. I simply refuse to support an industry that condones animal abuse. This choice has changed my life. This lifestyle doesn't only do me good, though. It's far beyond personal gain. The meat industry contributes greatly to climate change; animals raised for food account for more greenhouse gases than all the planes, cars, and trucks *combined*. A worldwide mindful diet would also resolve so much of the world's hunger. If we stopped growing crops exclusively for animals that will just end up on someone's dinner plate, we could feed the planet seven times over. . . . We could feed hungry PEOPLE with the crops we're growing for animals that we kill. Let that sink in.

This is where Karliin Brooks comes in. Karliin makes it easier for us all to be mindful eaters. She is the founder of The Squeeze, a 100 percent organic, raw, and gluten-free cold-press juice company in NYC. Now, I drink plenty of juices and smoothies, but Karliin's mission to bring healthy and compassionate alternatives to mass-produced junk foods resonated with me. Not only does her company provide fresh juices at numerous locations in the NYC area, but she also has an entire menu of raw comfort foods that are healthy for your body *and* for the planet. The Squeeze is committed to veg-ucating the world by advocating a lifestyle of kindness and cruelty-free products, all while serving up some nutritious food that's fresh and mostly locally-sourced. With this book, Karliin is helping people *everywhere* become mindful eaters, mindful of their own health and of our planet. This book isn't just about drinking green juice and calling it a day, it's about changing your lifestyle. It's about becoming aware of how everything you consume affects *all* life, not just yours. This book will help you get one step closer to being one with this amazing world we live in.

—Russell Simmons

INTRO

You may be thinking, *ugh, yet another cleansing-detox-diet-green-juice-hippie-bullshit book?! NO WHEY.*

Fine. A little bit yes, but mostly hell no.

This wondrous book *is* a book about cleansing recipes, but do yourself a favor and throw all your misinformed preconceptions about cleansing out the window. We'll take care of that later.

This most certainly isn't a diet book (*ew*). Diets imply all sorts of restrictions that are ultimately unrealistic for long-term, real life application.

Can we get real here?

YES, if you cleanse you'll most likely shed a few pounds and look damn fine in those jeans, but that's not the point, only a perk. The recipes in these are anti-diet food. They're sensual, satiating, and fresh (just like you, baby girl). They're feel good, look good food.

YES, there are green juice recipes in here. I mean, duh, what were you expecting?

Green juices are the ultimate babe fuel. Get that into your beautiful brain. They're not gross and there's no fucking way you could eat that many vegetables in a day if they weren't juiced. But babes are people too and they get peckish, which is why this book has the dreamiest Snaxxx recipes. Cue angelic, heavenly sound effects because who doesn't love snacks? FIve out of five humans agree that cleanse-friendly snack options get their blood pumping.* (*May not be a "real" statistic.) Snacks are awesome, that's that.

As far as *hippie bullshit*? I don't even know what that means . . . why would you say that?

This book *is* all about self-love . . . and not in the masturbatory sense, although that's cool too. The main goal here is to do you, and do you *really* well; to love and worship every single glorious part of yourself. It's about time to treat yo' self with cleansing foods that reclaim your prime!

You're (hopefully) a semi-aware, gorgeous human who understands that what you put inside your body (*wink wink*) affects your overall well-being. So why eat shitty foods?

Maybe you feel weirded out and intimidated by cleansing out, but RE-LAX. Regardless of your body type (probably hot, I just know it), experience, and knowledge, there's something in here for YOU.

EATING RA
CLEAN, AN
-WHY

W, EATING

D DETOXING

BOTHER?

GETTIN' DOWN & DIRTY WITH CLEANSING

A food cleanse is all about detoxifying your hot bod of shit that's caked on your insides, collected over years and years of nutritional neglect. Not quite literally, but still a similarly disgusting mental picture.

I'm totally open-minded about the things you might want inside of you, but toxins just aren't cute—they prevent your body from operating at full capacity. Try as it might, your body can't rid itself completely of present toxins when there are new loads constantly arriving.

While your wondrous body already does a pretty good job of eliminating a lot of toxins on its own, the purpose of a cleanse is to give it a goddamn break. The recipes in this book are meant to kickstart the detoxifying process, not replace it altogether.

These recipes are rich with nutrients and enzymes that are easily digestible and quickly absorbed by your body, allowing your cells to release toxins via your skin, lungs, kidneys, and other awesome organs. Easy digestibility is a big deal since digestion takes up most of your body's energy—so rather than having to digest, your bod can get to work detoxifying and making you a sexier human.

ARNING: THIS SHIT
S GROSS

TOXINS 101

Although toxins may seem like a mysterious buzzword, they're ubiquitous nowadays. Everything from food, pollution, alcohol, drugs, and even negative emotions can bring you down and flood your body with disease-causing toxins.

Like most products that are detrimental to your body, toxins aren't labeled with a WARNING: THIS SHIT'S GROSS FOR YOU sticker. Most of the body products we use contain toxins. Processed foods contain toxins. Even a stressful workday is toxic. In fact, everything is toxic on some level.

We can't all be bubble babies and stop living our lives just 'cause toxins are pervasive. Instead, you can educate yourself on toxins that you *can* control and limit your body's intake.

Don't be rude.

SOME JUICY CLEANSING ADVICE

This is not a crash diet! The point of this book, and altogether of a cleanse, isn't to "erase" a weekend of binge drinking, eating, or all of the above. You can't undo your McDonald's holiday pie-for-breakfast regimen with a cleanse; and you certainly can't expect to reverse years of poor habits with any of the foods in this book. I highly discourage you from sporadically cleansing and then returning to bad eating on a continuous basis. It's harmful to your nervous system to relentlessly yo-yo from cleanse to binge.

Pretty please, with raw organic sugar cane on top, don't use this book for that. Instead, use this book to refocus your eating habits to become the best YOU possible. Make occasional cleansing part of your long-term habits to help your body to detox. Take things slow and at your own pace!

Don't start off with an advanced cleansing menu if you've never cleansed before. Incorporate the recipes in this book into your routine, even if you're not cleansing. You'll slowly start to crave juices and other nutritional powerhouses. *Green juice as a snack? Don't mind if I do.* Hopefully, this book will teach you long-term habits that'll stick with you throughout your life. Remember, this is all about loving and taking care of yourself, *not* about restricting and punishing (unless you're into that). *Wink. Wink.*

WHY RAW?

All of the fabulous recipes in this book are RAW. Like, raw as in they're very good, but also they're literally raw and uncooked. Whether it's a juice recipe, chips, or even soup, everything in here is as raw as raw can be. So what does that even mean?

Keeping things raw is extremely beneficial for your health and it's the optimum way to get the most nutrients from food. When fruit and vegetables are cooked, most of their nutrients are killed by the cooking process. Eating raw foods is the best way for your body to make the most of enzymes, essential fatty acids, and minerals. Raw foods are gentler on digestion and naturally give you an energy boost. Not to mention, they're extremely easy and often cheap to prepare. I mean . . . you're cutting out A LOT of the prep time by simply bypassing the whole cooking part. With a little bit of planning, raw meals are a snap and will keep you going all day.

Raw foods consist of anything that is uncooked or kept below 118°F. Meaning, even soups can be raw. You can still eat your faves even if you're pursuing a cleaner diet. Wonderful tools like dehydrators are essential in keeping things RAWnchy. A dehydrator maintains a constant, low temp for a very long time so that it (surprise, surprise) removes moisture from food. It'll become your new BFF in this journey to clean-eating utopia.

Very cool, you may be thinking, *but why can't I use that giant thing in my kitchen also known as an oven instead of a dehydrator?* Well, darlings, most ovens' lowest temp is usually around 200°F . . . so that doesn't qualify as raw. While there are some keen tricks you can apply to your home oven to make its lowest temp even lower, a dehydrator is a great tool to have and that's what I use for all the recipes listed in this book.

WHY DETOX?

This is the part of the book where shit gets REAL.
There are endless benefits of detoxing. As long
as you're eating clean and eating right, your body
will be flooded with continuous perks. More often
than not, people are attracted to cleanses because
they have a weight loss goal in mind, and that's
OK, but that's not the point. Whether you're drawn
to a detox for its weight loss properties, I know
you'll stick around for the myriad other perks.

IT'S ALL ABOUT BALANCE

So much of detoxing has to do with balance. First, the way one gets into detoxing should be sensible. It's not beneficial or safe to flip-flop from cleansing to eating like shit the next week. All that will do for you is stress your nervous system. Detoxing is a form of balancing your body.

First, let's throw it back to grade school science and remind ourselves what ions are. An ion is either an element or mineral that has a positive or negative charge, meaning it either has too many or too few electrons. For our purposes, the difference between a positive-ionically charged substance and a negative-ionically charged substance is how absorbable it is by the body. So, what happens? The age-old saying: opposites attract, but *not* in a good way. The positive-ionically charged things you put into your body get stuck onto your negative-ionically charged body. And so it goes on and on until you eventually attempt to remove what shouldn't be there to begin with. The more shit you intake, the more that's glued into your body. When that happens, your pH levels are lowered and your body becomes less efficient because it's encumbered with layer upon layer of debilitating toxins.

Whenever you consume negative-ionically charged foods, they attract the positive-ionically charged toxins to help flush them out. Juicing, and overall cleansing, loosens up the layers of toxins and removes them. It's all about movement. A dynamic cellular system allows your body to become balanced, alkalized, and, ultimately, cleaner. Once the debilitating toxins are loosened up and purged, your metabolism is kickstarted and your body begins working at full capacity again (since it doesn't have to deal with all the toxic shit you purposefully put in it).

Alkalize: Having a pH of greater than 7

Most cleansers are able to, *ahem*, pass the purged toxins naturally, but sometimes if your gorgeous colon isn't strong enough, you may want to look into different methods. If you're deep into a juice cleanse and you suddenly begin to feel bogged down (if you feel tired, have headaches, and have general malaise), it's not the juicin' that's getting to you, it might be the toxins that are trapped in your body. A professional colonic is an amazing way to clean you out. If you're truly serious about detoxing, colonics are an essential part of it. But, remember to take things slow and first transition into a cleanse-friendly lifestyle.

ARE YOU READY FOR SOME GOOD OLE MATH?

Food, Alcohol, Drugs, Negative Emotions = Positive-Ionically Charged

and

The Human Body = Negative-Ionically Charged

Fruits and Vegetables = Negative-Ionically Charged

ALKALINE PH

CONSUME FREELY AND ALWAYS
STRENGTH + YOUTH

NUETRAL PH

7.356 IS OPTIMUM PH FOR
HUMAN BLOOD

ACIDIC PH

CONSUME SPARINGLY OR NEVER
STRESS + AGING

HIGH ALKALINE
IONIZED WATER

MOST TAP WATER

CUTTING THE CRAP

New mantra: *Taking care of your butt leads to a clean gut.*

The gateway to optimal wellness is to rearrange your plumbing. Constipation can become a source of depression, anxiety, and illness. Think about it . . . why does crapping your face off feel so good? Your gut generates dopamine and serotonin. Pooping on the *regs* is a big deal.

Let's get deeper into it . . .
Movement isn't only beneficial in flushing out toxins, but it improves your overall well-being. A good focus when working to improve your health is your gut. About 60 percent of your immune system is housed in your gut, so it seems only natural to pay some extra attention to what's going on in there. One of the best ways to do just that is to feed your body plant-based, nutrient-heavy, whole foods (kind of like the ones in this book . . .). This helps keep the good bacteria happy and the harmful bacteria at bay. Yes, you always hear about good bacteria, but it's totally a real thing and not just a yogurt commercial ruse. Eating clean, plant-based foods is a great start to taking care of your lovely gut, but you can also take it a step further and supplement your diet with probiotics. I'm not talking about pill-form anything, but straight up foods that are natural sources of probiotics, like garlic, artichokes, and fermented veggies. Decreasing your sugar intake will also yield a happy, good bacteria kind of gut. Drinking copious amounts of water is also recommended to keep things in flux and to help flush toxins the hell out. And, in the midst of all that, an occasional professional colonic will do absolute wonders to your welfare. As I always say, *there's nothing a hose and some water can't fix*. Just kidding. I don't say that . . . but maybe I'll start 'cause it's true. Taking care of your gut and keeping things dynamic will improve your immunity, digestion, skin, mental clarity, energy, and overall balance. Flushing out harmful toxins helps eliminate malabsorption, which allows our digestive tracts to provide nourishment to our vital organs.

Poop-Fection: What You're Leaving Behind

Your bowels say a lot about what's going on inside ya. Generally, stool is 75 percent water, 8 percent dead bacteria, 8 percent live bacteria, and 8 percent indigestible fiber. But a proper poo is large-ish, well-formed, not too dense, and light brown. It should definitely plop gently into the toilet bowl, not burst. You should be hella proud of a solid, smooth floater. If your stool is broken up in pieces, your colon may be irritated and your nutrition might be lackluster. Heavy poop, on the other hand, signifies that your body isn't absorbing and using nutrients from food in an optimum manner.

Don't worry, I will help you get your shit together. (No pun intended.) It all starts with drinking a minimum of 64 ounces of water or juice every day and making raw produce a staple in your diet.

SQUEEZING IT OUT: URINE THERAPY

Who knew that you're flushing down the best kind of detox therapy for your health? First thing's first: urine is not dirty. It's totally hygienic, so let's all relax about it. Unlike popular belief, urine is not waste that the body is excreting. The food we eat is eventually broken down into tiny, tiny molecules and absorbed into the intestinal wall and passed along into the bloodstream. Those tiny food molecules circulate your hot bod, passing through the liver where toxins are removed (and later excreted from the body as our good friend poop). This now detoxed blood with the tiny food molecules enters the kidney and are filtered through, which removes excess amounts of water, salts, and any other elements your body does not need at that time. These excess elements are collected in the kidney as a PURIFIED and STERILE liquid we call urine (pee, piss, whiz, golden showers, etc.). So, essentially urine is made up of whatever elements your body didn't need at that time—it is not waste. It's actually valuable stuff. Many of those excess elements in the urine have been found to be healing and immune-boosting when reintroduced into the body. Yes, "reintroduced into the body" is a nice way of saying drinking your own piss. Urine is anti-fungal, anti-microbial, and antioxidant. When urine is recycled, it cleanses the blood. It's been known to clear skin, heal cuts, resolve colds, and even fight major illnesses like cancer.

Dr. David Jubb, a health guru and urine therapy practitioner, explains how exactly to consume your urine:

1. Collect the urine in midstream into a clean cup or container. This needs to be done as cleanly as possible, so ladies: clean your vag beforehand. Add a drop of fresh urine to about 1 teaspoon of clean water in a sterile container. Cover and shake vigorously for 30 seconds. Take a drop from that mixture and add to another teaspoon of clean water and shake for 30 more seconds. Combine a drop of that solution and mix with about a teaspoon of 90 proof vodka (used as preservative). Place three drops of the final mixture under the tongue hourly until there is improvement of symptoms. As you begin to feel better, make sure to lengthen the intervals of consuming. After 3 days, stop treatment and only resume if relapse occurs or if your symptoms are static.

2. Or simply use fresh urine drops directly. Make sure to use fresh urine in its

natural state. Start off by taking 1 to 5 drops of morning urine on your first day of therapy. On the second day, take 5 to 10 drops of urine. On the third day, take 5 to 10 drops of urine in the morning and the same amount at night before you go to bed.

As your therapy progresses, you'll learn which method and the amount of urine that works for you. Listen to your body and adjust accordingly.

Got urine?

ENZYMES

Enzyme: a substance produced by a living organism a.k.a. proteins that help break down all the yummy food you put in that bod of yours.

We should all be thanking our enzymes *daily* for all the incredible shit they do for our bodies. Instead, most of us simply ignore them, *if* they even know what an enzyme is. Without getting too *Science Friday*, enzymes are a catalyst, or a substance that increases the chemical reaction without any permanent change, for essentially any function your body does. No small feat! At our youth, when our bodies are less polluted by toxins, enzymes are abundant

and your bod works at full capacity. However, (for most of us) the longer you live, the more toxins you accumulate and less enzymes stick around. The traditional American diet uses up a fat handful of enzymes for digestion, and those enzymes are not being replaced. That's where raw foods and juices come to the rescue! Raw foods are filled with live enzymes that are beneficial for your body. The more raw foods you eat, the more enzymes your body will take in and keep to perform at the capacity of its youthful days. You will see for yourself how much your metabolism will increase when your body is flooded with live enzymes. All of your body's functions perform at their peak when your body receives a constant supply of enzymes. Thus the importance of raw detoxing is pretty clear. A combo of juices and raw foods (cooked below 118° F) will keep you stocked with enzymes and keep your body working at its optimal levels. Dead, cooked food cannot sustain living beings!

DID YA KNOW?
Eating raw
and detoxing
is a great start
to healthier
digestion.

WHAT'S YOUR BIOLOGICAL AGE?

We all know our chronological age (thanks, calendars!), but do you know what your biological age is? Depending on your lifestyle and how well you've taken care of your precious body, your biological age can be much older than your chronological age. Hopefully it's younger though. Biological age is based on cellular and organ processes and your overall health. The trick to reversing your biological age is a combination of what we've already talked about: pH levels, elimination, and enzymes. If you keep your pH levels balanced by consuming raw foods and juices, consistently flush out toxins, and keep your enzyme levels high, your biological age will surely revert to your years of prime. *ME-OW*. Who knew the road to agelessness and beauty was so obvious? I did.

DIGESTION

If it seems like eating raw foods is the secret to feeling good about almost everything in your life, you're right. It's true. Eating raw, and consequently being a raw human, will make your digestion work like a charm. The key to owning your digestion isn't *only* keepin' it raw, but being mindful of which foods you consume and *when* you do so. One of the goals of cleanse-friendly foods is to give your body a break from intense digestion so it can focus on flushing out toxins, so consuming foods that are easy to digest and leave your body quickly is key. Health food should be defined by how quickly and thoroughly it can leave the body, not by its nutritional content. These wonder foods that the body can take in and quickly eliminate are referred to as *quick exit foods*, for pretty obvious reasons. Quick exit foods lead to healthy digestion and will alleviate constipation, gassiness, IBS, and other woes. Not to mention that consuming non-quick exit foods wastes body energy on digestion, slows immunity, and slows weight loss since the waste isn't being eliminated.

MAKE SURE TO FOLLOW THESE TIPS FOR SMOOTH SAILING:

- *Always* **consume fruit on an empty stomach!** Don't go poppin' a cherry after you've been chowing. Ideally, fruit should be consumed first thing in the morning, or at least three hours after a meal. Fruit takes around 20 to 30 minutes to pass through the stomach and if eaten with anything else, the fruit will ferment and cause not-so-great times for you.

- **Avoid hot food and cold food.** Warm food is totally cool, but not in any extremes since it suspends digestions and wastes precious body energy. Avoid very cold iced drinks since it can create mucous and digestive problems.

- **Drink your FOOD!** Your stomach doesn't have a set of chompers like you do, so help it out by chewing your food well. Digestion begins in your mouth with the saliva enzyme ptyalin, which converts food into useable nutrients. Chewing also lets you better *taste* your food and leads to more satisfaction after a meal. Scarfing food down never feels good, no matter how hungry or busy you are.

- **Chew your DRINK!** The process of chewing is what kickstarts digestion. Don't chug your juice, which will only induce air

babies. Burping is highly unwanted and unpleasant. Slowing things down allows you to savor the juice, and it enables your digestion to get started. Remember: digestion begins in your mouth.

- **Only eat when you're HUNGRY!** This may seem obvious, but how often do you just snack because you're bored or watching TV? Just don't. Wait until your mouth is watering and you're truly hungry. Trust me, food will taste even better and your digestion will thank you.

- **Don't OVEREAT!** Stop eating a meal *before* you feel full. You've heard that one before, right? Overeating leads to bloating and/or fatigue . . . ahem, remember *every* Thanksgiving ever! That's just not cute. Overeating can lead to disease and it can lower the blood near the digestive system, taking it away from the brain. You're often fuzzy after a giant meal and with good reason. Eating to 80 percent capacity is ideal.

- **Don't eat when you're SAD.** Don't eat when you're in pain, tired, or in any emotional distress! These states weaken the body and impede proper digestion, leading to your foe indigestion and causing toxins to accumulate. Always eat when you're hungry.

GETTING JIGGY, THANKS TO JUICE

Raw, vegan, and clean foods improve your sex drive, baby. As if good health wasn't reason enough, now you know that clean foods increase libido, so you can get your freak *on* faster, longer, and more often.

1. **You look good**. This one's pretty obvious: if you eat and juice well, you look good and if you look good, you *feel* good. Clean eating contributes to weight loss, clearer skin, and faster metabolism. The increase in vitamin C in one's diet contributes to higher collagen production that in turn increases the elasticity of your skin. Confidence matters in between the sheets and good food will get you there.

2. **Energy boost.** Cleaner diet is a natural way to increase your energy in the bedroom and everywhere else too. Fresh fruits and veggies provide more sustainable energy your hot bod can use, not so-called "energy" foods that will give you a crash. Munch on a banana so you have energy to much on another banana later on (*wink, wink*).

3. **Gets your blood pumping.** When compared to an omnivorous diet, raw and vegan foods increase blood circulation, *especially* downstairs . . .

4. **Sex vitamin.** So many clean foods like carrots, alfalfa sprouts, raspberries, and sweet potatoes contain vitamin E a.k.a. the sex vitamin. Vitamin E has been known to increase libido in both men and women, as well as heighten sensitivity and desire. How about you eat a handful of raspberries and we go somewhere private, huh?

5. **Taste better.** Clean eaters taste better! Believe me, I've done the research. Vegans, raw eaters, and clean dieters have been known to smell fresher than their meat-eating counterparts. The high-water content of a clean diet also increases lubrication, which increases the fun. Finally, certain foods make your bodily fluids taste better...*ahem,* pineapple anyone?

TOOLS, METHODS, INGREDIENTS & ADVICE

In this section you'll find everything you need to succe-sex-fully use this book! From the tools needed, to questions you may have while cleansing—WE GOT YOUR BACK.

DON'T BE A TOOL,
USE A REALLY GOOD ONE

By far the most important tool you'll need to use this book is *drumroll* a juicer, duh. There are plenty of juicers out there in the juicin' sea, but they all generally fall into one of three categories: centrifugal, masticating, and twin gear. Let's get into the nitty-gritty, shall we?

CENTRIFUGAL

This is your run-of-the-mill juicer you'll most likely encounter first when Googling the word "juicer." It's the cheapest option of juicers, but not necessarily the best one. It works by quickly spinning a metal blade against a mesh filter, thus separating juice from its pulp. The biggest con is that the fast-spinning blade generates heat that can destroy some of the enzymes in the juice. The heat also oxidizes nutrients, yielding in a less nutritious juice.

MASTICATING

To masticate means to chew (your food, hopefully), and that's just what this baby does. Masticating juicers yield juice by grinding your produce, similar to how your chompers chew. They produce way less heat than a centrifugal juicer, but cost a bit more.

TWIN GEAR (ALSO KNOWN AS COLD-PRESS)

Like the name suggests—twin gear juicers function with two overlapping gears that work together to extract the maximum amount of juice from produce. They operate at a slower speed than other juicers, but slow and steady wins the race: this causes minimum nutrient oxidation, meaning the juice it yields contains the most nutrients and stays that away for longer. This one's for the committed

health babes as it is the priciest model of them all. As the saying goes: with great $$$, comes great juice-ability. The type of juicer you get is entirely up to you, but give it some serious thought. Think about your commitment to juicing and why you're juicing in the first place. Yes, a great juicer can be pricey, but in the long run its nutritional benefits far outweigh the monetary value.

TIPS:

- Wash and soak produce even if you plan on peeling it!
- Use soaked produce within 1 to 2 days, otherwise it might become mushy.
- Make sure produce is completely dry before storing it.
- Remember to soak softer produce (strawberries, peaches, leafy greens) for less time than firmer produce.
- Alternatively, you can spray your produce with a water and vinegar mixture and let sit for 5 minutes before rinsing.

TOOLS CHECKLIST

FOOD PROCESSOR (such as a *Cuisinart*)

HIGH-SPEED BLENDER (such as *a Vitamix)* that is all-purpose and can tackle soups, nut butters, smoothies, mylks, dressings, etc.

COFFEE GRINDER to grind small amounts of nuts, seeds, and dehydrated veggies.

DEHYDRATOR (such as *Excalibur)* for all your bread, cracker, cake, and pizza needs.

CHEF'S KNIFE for cutting the bigger and harder (whoa now, focus) produce into juice-appropriate pieces.

PARING KNIFE to have when prepping citrus for juicing.

MANDOLINE for thinly slicing any veggies and fruits.

STRAINER/COLANDER to easily drain or squeeze out excess liquids in produce.

NUT MILK BAG Strainer/colander to easily drain or squeeze out excess liquids in produce.

NON-SLIP WOODEN CUTTING BOARD for all the cutting, mah dear. We like wood. Plastic isn't eco-friendly, plus wood is cleaner and has natural antibacterial properties.

A LARGE BASIN/KITCHEN SINK for properly washing produce.

BIODEGRADABLE PLASTIC BAG to line your juicer's pulp basket for easy clean up (if your juicer has a pulp basket). Not necessary, but helpful to have.

MASON JARS/GLASS CONTAINERS to store your ready-to-drink juice.

For more information on where to find these tools, see the Resources section (page 423).

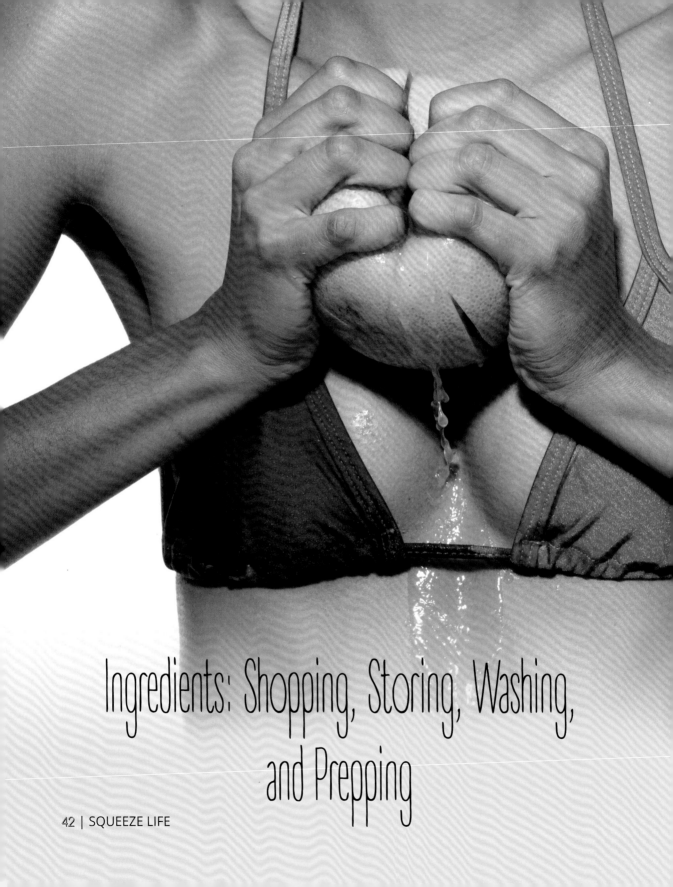

Ingredients: Shopping, Storing, Washing, and Prepping

GETTING SHIT CLEAN—
WASHING, SOAKING & PREPPING

Properly washing produce is a crucial step of juicing, and holding an apple under the running faucet for 10 seconds and rubbing it halfheartedly doesn't count. You shouldn't even rub anything halfheartedly. Unwashed produce can be contaminated with bacteria and traces of pesticide— *especially* those of the nonorganic variety— and can lead to foodborne illnesses.

"Juice today, you'll save on doctor's visits tomorrow."

- Place the produce in your kitchen sink or a large basin and add enough purified water to cover it completely.
- Add a few generous splashes of apple cider vinegar and allow produce to chill out for at least 5 minutes (and for up to 15 minutes).
- Make sure to stir the produce around a bit during the soaking time— agitation is helpful in cleaning it.
- Use a designated produce-only brush to gently scrub fruits/veggies.
- Rinse with water
- Allow to dry on a tea towel or gently pat dry before storing or use.

PREPPING CITRUS

When juicing lemons, limes, oranges, and grapefruits:

- Cut a sliver off the top and bottom of your citrus, so it sits on its own and doesn't roll away.
- Using a knife, start at the top and peel the rind away, but make sure to keep as much of the white pith as possible since it is filled with nutrients and antioxidants.
- Segment the citrus.

You're ready to juice that citrus, baby! FYI: some recipes in this book do require the entire citrus rind be included, but the directions will say so, so make sure to read carefully.

SHORT CUT: Fruit and veggie washes can remove those nasty pesticides, waxes, and harsh chemicals! My favorite is Trader Joe's Fruit & Vegetable Wash.

SOAKING YER NUTS (AND SEEDS)

There will be lots of nuts in the recipes listed in this book, so knowing how to handle 'em is essential. Now how you do so in your personal life is entirely up to you, but in this book, we have some guidelines. Soaking nuts or seeds removes enzyme inhibitors, and improves digestibility and texture. It basically unlocks the nut's maximum potential. Simply add your nuts/seeds to a large bowl, fill with enough purified water to cover, and place a breathable cloth towel over the bowl. Allow to soak for the suggested time. Make sure to soak nuts/seeds well before dehydrating for 12 to 24 hours, until nice and crispy. Yes, that seems like a crazy long time, but simply make dehydrating nuts part of your food prep routine! Dehydrate large batches at a time, so you can always have them available for recipes (and snacking, let's be real). If you don't dehydrate your nuts/seeds, they can become moldy.

If you don't have this chart handy with ya, a good rule of thumb is the harder the nut, the longer the soaking time. Store your nuts in an airtight glass container in a cool, dark place or in the fridge.

DID YA KNOW? Nuts and seeds are amazing little thangs! They contain phytic acid, a type of phosphorus that acts as a protective barrier. Basically, the phytic acid keeps the seeds from germinating until the right time, but the phytic acid isn't for human consumption. It binds to the gastrointestinal tract and often causes irritation when consumed sans soaking. Soaking mimics nature and enables the nuts and seeds to slowly release said elements that are otherwise irritants for human digestions. So make sure to soak yer nuts, will ya?

SOAKING TIMES:
A MINI NUT CHART

cashews: 2 to 4 hours
flax seeds: no soaking necessary
hemp seeds: no soaking necessary
sesame seeds: no soaking necessary
macadamias: 2 to 4 hours
pistachios: 2 to 4 hours
pumpkin seeds: 2 to 4 hours
sunflower seeds: 2 to 4 hours
pecans: 4 to 6 hours
walnuts: 6 to 8 hours
hazelnuts: 6 to 8 hours
almonds: 8 to 12 hours

REDIENTS

Throughout the recipes in this book, you may encounter an ingredient you're not super familiar with . . . like, what the hell is Irish moss gel? Don't you worry now, this section will come in handy for those moments. Check the Resources section for more tips on where to find these ingredients.

PRODUCE

Breaking down any weirdo fruit or veg
that you may not be so solid on.

AÇAI:

Hailing from Central and South America, this little fruit is famed for being a superfood . . . and with good reason. It's jam-packed with antioxidants, way more than most other berries. Amino acids and omega fatty acids are also abundant in this berry, which helps slooooow down the aging process.

ALOE VERA:

You're probably already familiar with aloe vera's benefits for your sumptuous skin, but aloe vera juice is just as wondrous. It contains tons of amino acids, vitamins, and minerals so it's incredibly beneficial for the cleansing process. It's soothing and anti-inflammatory, boosts your immune system, and it contains vitamins that promotes healthy hair growth. Not too shabs, eh? You can probably find it at your local grocery store or where they sell plants.

COCONUT MEAT:

Coconut meat adds a creamy richness to tons of recipes, and it's a great way to mimic the *feel* of dairy in clean foods. It's hydrating and amazing for your skin. I recommend buying them at well-stocked health stores (usually frozen) or buying young Thai coconuts whole. If buying whole coconuts, make sure that they are fresh and have not been treated with any preservatives.

COCONUT WATER:

Coconut water should never be pasteurized! Make sure you buy good quality coconut water, usually found at well-stocked health food stores. You can buy it frozen or fresh.

DANDELION GREENS:

Dandy greens are known for being a pesky herb that's invading your lawn, but they're actually extremely healthful. They are totally crammed with vitamin K, which is known to strengthen yer lazybones. Additionally, it offers vitamin A, fiber, and an alphabet of other essential vitamins. If you don't find them at your local grocery store, check out a more health-oriented, natural market.

JICAMA:

Jicama is a bulbous root veg with thick, brown skin that's mild and slightly sweet. It's low in calories, antioxidant, and anti-inflammatory. It blends really well in any green juice for extra added benefits that will go essentially untasted. Find it at most grocery stores.

PANTRY ITEMS

These are all your "pantry" ingredients, meaning anything that doesn't fall under the produce category.

RAW AGAVE NECTAR:

Agave nectar is a natural sweetener known as aguamiel, or honey water, in Mexico. It's made by extracting the sap from the blue agave's core, filtering it and heating it over low temperature until it transforms into its syrupy form. It has a low glycemic index and it's rich with vitamins C, D, and E. You can most likely buy it at your local grocery store, but make sure to look for a raw variety.

BRAGG LIQUID AMINOS:

Bragg Liquid Aminos is produced by the healthy-pioneering Bragg fam. It's a liquid protein concentrate made from soybeans that contains 16 naturally-occurring amino acids. It's similar in taste to soy sauce and it is actually used to replace soy sauce in most recipes. Purchase it in health stores, some local grocery stores, or online.

RAW CACAO:

Raw cacao is powdered chocolate in its purest form; also see cacao nibs. It's milled in a low temperature so it retains its nutrients, such as magnesium and iron. It can be used to make sweets, smoothies, and raw "baked" goods. Perfect for those insanely sinful chocolate cravings that take over our minds from time to time.

CACAO NIBS:

Cacao nibs are essentially chocolate in its purest form. They're dried and fermented nibs of the cacao beans, and taste mildly bitter, nutty, and chocolaty. Cacao nibs can be used to accentuate chocolate flavas and add an extra crunch; they're also a great source of antioxidants, fiber, magnesium, and iron. You can find them in specialty grocery stores and online.

CHIA SEEDS:

Chia seeds are from a flowering plant that's related to mint. It's a tasteless nutritional powerhouse that is most commonly used as a thickening agent in oatmeals, puddings, smoothies, and a variety of vegan recipes. They're an excellent source of omega-3 fat, soluble fiber, calcium, magnesium, phosphorus, manganese, and protein. They can be purchased at most local grocery stores or any health market. Make sure to grind or soak them before use for ultimate digestibility.

CHLORELLA:

I'll admit it, this all-natural supplement does sound like a disease, but I promise you it's quite the opposite. Chlorella is a freshwater algae that is rich with amino acids, chlorophyll, beta-carotene, potassium, phosphorus, biotin, magnesium, and a range of B-vitamins. It's extremely detoxifying and has been proven to negate the effects of radiation.

COCONUT BUTTER:

Coconut butter is made by pureeing the whole meat of the coconut into a creamy, luscious butter. It's creamier and closer to butter than coconut oil. You can find it at most health food stores.

COCONUT NECTAR:

Coconut nectar is on the same wavelength as maple syrup. It's made from the naturally sweet and nutrient-dense sap that comes from coconut trees. It's low-glycemic and contains 17 amino acids, vitamin C, and has an almost neutral pH level. You can find it in most health food stores.

COCONUT OIL:

Coconut oil is the extracted oil from the meat of coconuts. It's often used in edible applications, but it can also be part of a healthy skincare routine. It's abundant in antioxidants, healthy fatty acids, lauric acid, and it has antifungal properties. Virgin coconut is lowest in cholesterol and saturated fats. You can find a variety of coconut oils at your local grocery store nowadays.

COCONUT SUGAR:

Coco sugar comes from the coconut palm tree, and it's better to consume than your standard refined sugar. Its glycemic levels are lower than other sugars and it even contains some nutrients. NUTRIENTS! . . . In sugar . . . Look at the world we live in! You'll find iron, zinc, calcium, potassium, and some antioxidants in coconut sugar which are reason enough to transition over to the sweeter side of natural sweeteners.

DATES:

. . . and I'm not talking about the kind you want to leave in the morning. Dates are a great sweetener in many recipes in this book. They yield a thick and almost caramel-like flavor and texture, but better yet, they're rich with essential nutrients, vitamins, and minerals, including dietary fiber, antioxidant tannins, iron, potassium, calcium, and much more. You can buy them anywhere, they're not that weird.

FERMENTED BROWN RICE PROTEIN:

For the meat-free babes, this is a welcomed form of protein. It's lean and low-fat, low-sugar, low glycemic, and it promotes muscle recovery. Mix into smoothies, oatmeal, or sneak it into desserts.

FLAXSEEDS:

These guys are one of the oldest fiber crops ever, and they're one of the most beneficial, too. They boast a hefty amount of dietary fiber, manganese, vitamin B_1, and the essential fatty omega-3. They're great thickening agents; mix them in smoothies, puddings, and oatmeal for a instant thick texture. Make sure to grind them before using for ultimate digestibility.

GOJI BERRIES:

This tart, yet sweet little berry packs a punch when it comes to fighting those free radicals which cause us to age. These berries are full of antioxidants, beta-carotene, protein, and vitamin A. Top them on your morning cereals or smoothies. You can also use them in savory salads for a sweet bite! I even sneak them into the movies instead of candy or popcorn, shhhhh.

HEMP SEEDS:

Hemp seeds come from a different species of the infamous cannabis plant. Rather than getting you high, these seeds are a rich source for protein, essential fats, and fiber. Among its many nutritional benefits are weight loss, lowered cholesterol, an improved immune system, and blood sugar control, just to name a few. Sprinkle them over smoothies, oatmeal, or incorporate them into raw breads and crackers. Buy them at your natural health market or online. Make sure to grind them before use for ultimate digestibility.

IRISH MOSS GEL:

Irish moss is unprocessed and raw seaweed that can be used as a thickening agent in cooking. Use it anywhere you want a thick, smooth consistency. This weird stuff contains antioxidants, ionic minerals, and it's been known to soothe the digestive tract. Buy it at a natural foods market or online.

LACUMA POWDER:

Lacuma is a tropical fruit native to Peru. In this book, we use the powder from that fruit. It's a low-glycemic sweetener that contains beta-carotene, iron, zinc, vitamin B_3, calcium, and protein. It is rich and maple-like in taste and a great way to halt your refined sugar intake.

MACA:

Maca is a root from the radish fam and it can most often be found in powder form. This supplement is very powerful and you should take it slow . . . start off with gentle amounts and don't exceed more than 1 tablespoon a day. It provides plenty of vitamins B, C, and E, calcium, zinc, iron, magnesium, and phosphorus. It boosts libido for ladies and gents,

provides an energy boost and can be used to balance your mood. It's a damn sexy root if there ever was one.

MISO:

Miso is a popular Japanese ingredient that's made by fermenting soybeans, barley, brown rice, and other grains with a type of (healthful) fungus to create a salty and probiotic paste. Miso introduces umami to any dish it's used on, in addition to being incredible for your intestines (thanks to its probiotic properties). It's also a good source of antioxidants, vitamins B, and amino acids. It's important that you purchase organic, mellow white miso! You can most likely find it at your local grocery store or Asian markets.

SALT:

When we refer to salt in these recipes, we highly suggest using Himalayan pink sea salt that's finely ground. This kind of salt is one of the purest salts available that contains essential minerals

that support detox and pH regulation and increases circulation. You can find it at most health food stores.

TURMERIC:

Magical turmeric has been around for quite a long time in Chinese and Indian culture as a medicinal spice. It comes from the curcuma longa plant and it is distinct due to its bright orange-yellow hue. It contains potent anti-inflammatory and antioxidant properties and it's been known to reduce the risk of a variety of cancers. It's peppery, warm, and slightly bitter in flavor. You can either purchase it as a powder or fresh root (it looks similar to a ginger root). Buy it at your local health food store.

VANILLA:

There are lots of ways to get vanilla flavor in a recipe; the ones that we use in this book are alcohol-free vanilla extract, vanilla beans, and/or vanilla paste. Vanilla extract is made by seeping vanilla beans in some mixture of water or alcohol. For

these recipes, we recommend using good quality alcohol-free vanilla extract. It's a splurge but the difference is significant. Vanilla beans are a great option, but they can get pricey. Make sure you use fair trade vanilla beans. Vanilla paste is a puree of vanilla beans and some type of sweetener. It's a happy medium between vanilla extract and actual vanilla beans. For the purposes of these recipes, 1 teaspoon of vanilla extract is equal to a 2-inch piece of vanilla bean (meaning 1 typical vanilla bean will equal 3 teaspoons extract). Vanilla paste is used the same way as vanilla extract.

NUTRITIONAL YEAST:

Perhaps my favorite ingredient with the most lewd name, nutritional yeast is actually a gift to those keeping clean diets. It's made from saccharomyces cerevisiae, a single-cell organism that grows on molasses and unlike regular yeast, it isn't activated so it doesn't have the power to leaven. Best part is that

it tastes like cheese. Find it at specialty health stores or at bulk stores.

DID YA KNOW? Making vanilla paste is easy and you can have total control of your ingredients, which is always a very good thing! Slice 6 vanilla beans in half lengthwise and allow them to air dry for about 2 days. Once dried out, pulse them in the food processor until they turn into a powder. Add ½ cup of agave nectar and continue pulsing until totally blended. Strain to catch any larger chunks. Store in a clean, airtight jar in the refrigerator indefinitely. Use it just like you use vanilla extract.

CLEANSING GUIDES

Unless I'm in the bedroom, I don't like telling people what to do. Just live your life how it bests suits you, babe. But if you're not sure how to approach a cleanse or if you just like a little more structure in your life, these guides are here for ya. Remember, these are *guides* not requirements. You know yourself best, so listen to that hot bod of yours and if something isn't working, feel free to change it up. Always consult with a professional if you have any major health concerns.

We're not into a *one size fits all* approach when cleansing. Everybody is different, so all of our cleanses are fully customizable to best suit each unique, gorgeous snowflake that's planning on cleansing out. Regardless of which level you begin with, remember to *always* mix up your juices and smoothies for optimum nutrient benefits. If you drink the same recipes every day, you're depriving yourself of an entire rainbow of fruits and veg, and a whole freaking alphabet of vitamins. So change it up, will ya?

LEVEL I: BASIC BITCH

Level I is a beginner cleanse, ideal for babes who are new to cleansing or someone who's looking to add more clean greens in their lives. It's so very important you don't shock your body by starting with a more advanced cleanse and going full throttle if you're brand spankin' new to the plant-based lifestyle. It's okay to take baby steps! In no time, your babe-alicious bod will be ready to take it to the maxxx. The idea for this cleanse level is to try out an all-raw, -clean, and -vegan diet. Meaning, you can eat or drink *ANYTHING* in this entire damn book.

You call this cleansing?

Hell yeah we do. You can eat this way until 6 p.m. every day or only on Mondays. Eat this way for one day a week, or for an entire week. Or for a month. Do it for a dare, do it 'cause you care. Who knows? Maybe you'll end up eating this way for the rest of your life (I'm crossing my fingers for ya). The main point here is to eat and drink as much plant-based nosh as you can, and move away from animal by-products and processed foods. This is an intro to the amazing world of the RAWnchy life!

With this cleanse level you should eat as you normally would, simply replace all that gnarly gunk with *good-for-you* grub featured throughout this book. Just by introducing a variety of plant-based foods, fruit and veg juices, smoothies, and raw snaxxx throughout your day, you're already radically cleansing your body from toxins that are so prevalent in animal by-products and processed shit. We even included a bunch of tonics, elixirs, mylks, and spritzes to round out your menu and satiate the heck out of you. *No one* will know you are eating clean, unless you tell 'em. This means you don't have to hide away while you cleanse and rev up your metabolism! Get your friends over and feed them, pour 'em a drink, and be sexy as fuck together. This cleanse isn't about making your life harder! While this level includes *ALL* the food recipes in this book, feel free to juice it up or make any smoothies too. Mix it up, stuff your face, *and* feel hella good—that's the plan here. There's zero deprivation allowed. Even if you only eat the snaxxx and a few smoothies for a week, you'll *still* feel better than with a cheeseburger and fries.

SAMPLE MENU:

What your menu might look like if you cleanse with Level I for a day.

Rise & shine: SUPERcharged Cinnamon Oatmeal (page 378)

Snaxxx time: Raspberry-Chia Fruit Roll Up (page 398) OR a handful of Cocoa-loco Almonds (page 388)

Midday meal: Summer Dreamin' Rolls page 338) OR Banana Bread if you're feelin' like a liquid lunch (page 242)

Need another snaxxx? That's cool: Fancy Almond Mylkyway (page 206) or any other Mylk

Last meals: Creamy Butternut Squash Soup (page 328) or Faux-lafel (page 344)

That's just *ONE* possibility out of the hundreds of recipes here. You can adjust according to your preferences, schedule, whatever ya want!

SIDE EFFECTS:

If you're a cleanse virgin, you might experience some side effects that are not a big deal, but it's important to know what's going on with your bod.

HEADACHES

Headaches can happen if you completely give up or reduce how much caffeine you consume daily. Remember to drinks *LOTS* of water when you're cleansing (but really, just in generai). You can use soothing lavender to relax you (dab some lavender oil on your temple).

GOT STOMACH PROBS?

These recipes are fiber powerhouses and if you're not accustomed to intaking that much fiber, you may experience some stomach cramps. Remember to slowly introduce new foods to your body so it has time to adjust to it. If you eat like shit and suddenly become a fiber-maniac, you'll *feel* it. Find the right amount of fiber that's right for you and slowly build up from that.

CRAZY CRAVINGS

Cravings are kind of not real. They're all in your head. Cleansing is all about baby steps so your bod can adjust to it, but you should also mentally prepare yourself. Set yourself up for success! Use the buddy system—who doesn't want to get clean and sexy with a friend? Don't get bored! Plan a busy schedule when you're cleansing, that way you don't have time to fixate on cravings. Eating on the reg or adding more protein can also help any hunger pains!

I GOTTA GO

Are you peeing more than usual? Don't worry, that's a good thing. The more you pee, the more toxins you get rid of.

DAMN, YOU'RE LOOKING GOOD

You look *so* happy! Have you lost weight? Your skin is glowing! *YUP.* You'll hear a lot of that. When you begin to eat clean, you'll have more energy, lose weight, and probably sleep sounder. Your bod will slowly adjust to new healthy habits and you won't miss any processed foods.

WHAT NOW:

The idea with Level I is to introduce clean eating to your daily routine, but if you're "done" with a cleanse, remember that you should *TAKE IT SLOW.* Don't head off to Chipotle to celebrate and chow down on a giant burrito baby. If you're craving that something something, eat a tiny amount of it to reintroduce your body to it . . . that's not ideal, but we know how it is. I truly hope that once you begin to eat clean, you'll understand that turning back isn't an appealing option. You'll only feel better from here! When you get more adventurous, you can start moving up to our Level II cleanse.

LEVEL II: GIVE IT TO ME HARDER

With Level II you're officially taking it up a notch. Can I get a *hell yes*? Good for you, babe! This cleanse is all about giving your digestive system a damn, and much deserved, break. It works harder than anyone you know, seriously. There are no solid foods in this section. Don't panic, though! There are *tons* of delish juices and hearty smoothies for you to indulge in. This stuff is babe fuel to the MAXXX! But, if you're *really* feelin' it in a not-so-great way, you can totally make a soup. *Shhh, we won't tell anyone*.

Level II is ideal for more intermediate cleansers, meaning the good-looking folks who are already into plant-based or clean eating, but maybe not full-time (yet). The same advice from Level I goes with this cleanse: don't start full throttle if your body isn't accustomed to eating CLEAN. You'll only shock your system and feel shitty . . . and most likely not want to cleanse anymore because you think cleanses aren't good. Baby steps are the key to babe-hood! You'll get there. Maybe you'll start replacing your meal with one of the smoothies from this level for a few weeks before trying this out full-on. You can even incorporate juices and smoothies into your reg diet. Ideally, you'll move up to this level from Level I after you slowly start replacing the solid fare with some liquid gold.

This cleanse omits foods like:

- Nuts
- Oats
- Grains
- Any other fibrous foods that are hard to digest

Even if they are blended into a smoothie, make sure to stay away from those ingredients to *truly* give your system a break!

For this bad boy cleanse, you'll drink:
3 SMOOTHIES + 4 JUICES +
1 MYLK + PLENTY OF H_2O

Think of it this way: the smoothies are the meals, juices are snaxxx, and mylk is your dessert. You can drink your mylk whenever you like to. If you're into something sweet in the evening, wait all day and drink yo' precious in the evening. Make sure to drink plenty o' H_2O in between all the other bevs. Bonus points if you add a squeeze of lemon to your water! Maker sure to stay active, 'cause boredom is the enemy of cleansing. Do take it easy on yourself, though. This is *not* the time to learn kickboxing or train for a marathon, *especially* if you're slowly transitioning to a new cleanse intensity.

SAMPLE MENU:

What your menu might look like if you cleanse with Level II for a day.

This cleanse is highly adaptable to YOUR schedule, so there are no "set" meals or times. Simply drink when you're hungry. I suggest starting off your day with some lemon added to hot water—it'll kickstart your metabolism.

From there, it's really up to you as long as you keep with the plan: 3 smoothies as meal replacements, 4 juices as snaxxx, 1 mylk as a sweet treat, and plenty of water in between.

It's important to change up your smoothies and juice every day! Try to drink a different color for every meal, that way you're getting a variety of nutrients, rather than the same thing every day.

SIDE EFFECTS:

From here on up, you'll mostly experience some pretty bangin' side-effects.

Depending on how adjusted your system is to cleansing, you still might experience some of the not-so-fun side effects listed on Level I, but mostly you'll be feeling good.

WEIGHT LOSS

Yeah, you might drop one or more pants sizes . . . is that a problem?

GLOWIN'

The increase of antioxidants in your diet will contribute to your skin looking smoother, fresher, and exuding an overall babe glow.

IMMUNE BOOST

Most clean foods contain essential vitamins and minerals to support a healthy and active immune system. You'll prob heal faster from injuries and *not* feel sick. Headaches, digestion problems, and malaise will be a thing of the past.

HEALTHY HABITS

As your bod begins to adjust to a clean and compassionate lifestyle, you'll develop some pretty great habits. You won't crave toxic foods! You'll learn more about giving your body what it needs, rather than eating with your eyes.

SEX KITTEN

As you begin to feel better about yourself, your confidence will get a boost. You'll feel lighter, more capable, and sexy as fuck so you can . . . *erm,* get it ON. Clean eating contributes to a higher sex drive and an overall healthier sex life, so get your drink on and then get your freak on.
As you begin to turn into a liquid, plant-based goddess/god, you can slowly transition to our sexiest level yet. . . .

LEVEL III: BADDEST BITCH

With Level III you're officially a liquid babe, pouring down juice in all the right places. That's right, this level is juice-only. This is our most intense cleanse yet, but fear not! We promise your hot bod will have bragging rights. When you're through with this cleanse, your digestive tract will be renewed and rejuvenated. This level is for experienced juiceheads *only*. Don't you dare start here if you're a clean food virgin . . . seriously! This is the only time that it's cool to say

NO   VIRGINS   ALLOWED.

For this sultry cleanse, you 'll indulge in:

ANY 6 JUICES + TONS OF H_2O! Don't even look at the rest of the book. Start your juicer and only go forward! Remember to play around with as many of these recipes as you can, rather than sticking with your fave three, and only drinking them. Try to make *all* juices different colors every day. The more you experiment, the more you have fun (that's straight up life advice, not just juicing).

WARNING: You may notice higher energy levels, a sexy ass glow in your skin, and all around vibrance. Drink with caution.

SIDE EFFECTS:

If you're doing this right, you shouldn't really be experiencing many negative side effects. Unless you ignored our advice and simply jumped into this section without first adjusting your body, you shouldn't really be experiencing negative side effects. From here on, the only side effects are clarity, energy, strength, and lots of playtime.

SAMPLE MENU:
What your menu might look like if you cleanse with Level III for a day.

This cleanse is hella customizable! You can pick from any of the 50+ juice recipes in this book, as long as you switch it up and alternate between all of them. I recommend 6 serving of juice each day. Remember: drink a rainbow a day! As always, make sure you're drinking lots of water while cleansing, that way you help your bod flush out your system.

FINAL WORD

The most important thing when taking on a cleanse and/
or new diet is to take baby steps. It takes time for your body
to adjust to something new, so please proceed with that
in mind. If you've never cleansed before and your diet is
not at all clean and plant-based, then take some weeks to
adjust and slowly introduce clean foods from this book into
your lifestyle. Make things easier on yourself and prepare
for a cleanse in a way that'll set you up for success!
Always listen to your body. You know what feels right and
what doesn't. If you're not feeling so hot while undertaking
any of these levels in the correct way, and if you've
adjusted accordingly, then take a step back and regroup.
Make sure to take it slow! If you jump into something
before you're ready, you'll end up feeling not so great
and think that you simply can't cleanse. EVERYBODY CAN
CLEANSE! These cleanses are totally customizable and you
can adjust them to what best supports your lifestyle.
The goal is to be happy, treat your body right, and
transition into a clean and compassionate life.

ICON KEY FOR RECIPES

- **LEVEL I:** If yer a basic bitch to cleansing, look out for these recipes. Don't worry, you're still fabulous, and on your way to becoming even more so!

- **LEVEL II:** Indulge in all these recipes on the Level II cleanse.

- **LEVEL III:** You've made it! As THE baddest bitch around, enjoy these recipes on the Level III cleanse.

- **Anti-inflammatory**: These recipes help your bod keep its response to infections at bay—especially those suffering from rheumatoid arthritis.

- **Low-glycemic:** Recipes that won't spike your blood sugar levels.

- **Skin + beauty:** Recipes ideal for cell rejuvenation, containing tons of vitamins and nutrients meant to refresh and enhance your natural beauty, especially skin and hair.

- **Nut free:** Free of nuts.

TONS OF RECIPES

JUICES, ELIXIRS, AND MYLKS

[LOW GLYCEMIC JUICE]

These juices are all lean, keen(ky), and mostly green nutrient powerhouses. They're more veg-concentrated with some fruit here and there. They're all, however, crazy good and incredibly hydrating for your cute lil' organs. These juices are ideal for cleansing, but also a smart addition to your daily diet.

Red Pepper Refresher

This juice is an IRL (that means in real life, grandma) refresh button. Make it, drink it, love it, and reset your body back on track when you're feeling a little out of sorts. This combo is like a hearty soup, but in an extremely convenient format. Raw red peps are antioxidant bombs that promote healthy iron absorption, reduce bloating, and can kick-start thermogenesis, which increases your metabolism.

INGREDIENTS:

1 red bell pepper
1 cucumber
1 head broccoli
1 carrot
2 stalks celery
½ cup jicama, peeling optional
½ lime, unpeeled
1 handful of fresh basil
½ chili pepper

DIRECTIONS:

Wash all produce well. Cut all ingredients into juice-able pieces, process through juicer, and feel good.

stay CALM cuke ON

DID YA KNOW? A juice is never blended, that's a smoothie, yo! Make all juice recipes using a juicer, that way the pulp is extracted and you're left with nutrient dense . . . juice. A smoothie is made with a blender and is a great meal replacement that's rich with nutrients and fiber. Different strokes for different folks!

1 SERVING — LEVEL III, LG, SB, AI, LG

This juice is so incredibly refreshing I'm quenched just thinking about it. It's as calming as putting cucumber slices on your eyes, but jacked up to the max. Cucumber's high water content is great for hydrating yourself but also your organs (they need love too). Cukes also have soothing properties and make for some smooth skin. Parsley is known to boost your immune system, keep them ole bones strong, and it supports your kidneys by flushing out excess liquids.

INGREDIENTS:

½ lime, peeled
½ cucumber
½ cup zucchini (optional, makes a creamier juice)
½ handful of parsley
½ to 1 cup green grapes
Pinch of sea salt

DIRECTIONS:

Wash your produce well and cut into juice-able chunks. Process all ingredients through the juicer.

50 Shades of Green

This juice is naughty cause it tastes sooo good. Basil is anti-microbial, anti-fungal, anti-viral, and anti-inflammatory. All these "antis" keep your immune system spotless. This juice is filled with rich minerals, silica, potassium, and magnesium, which make it fabulous for your skin, hair, nails, and any skin-related complications. Drink away, darling!

INGREDIENTS:
1 cucumber
1 lime, only ½ peeled
1 apple
1 small handful of basil

DIRECTIONS:
Wash all produce well. Cut ingredients into juice-able pieces and process through juicer.

BE KIND
TO ANIMALS
OR
I'LL KILL YOU

oh, honey do!

1 SERVING — LEVEL III, LG, AI, SB

I love the combo of sweet and refreshing honeydew, creamy zucchini, and spicy watercress (especially on a hot summer's day)! Watercress is said to have cancer-preventative properties and it's also rich in antioxidants, vitamins A, C, and K. Honeydew's high water content makes it super effective at fighting high blood pressure levels, not to mention incredibly refreshing and hydrating.

INGREDIENTS:

1 zucchini
Handful of watercress
Handful of cilantro
1 cucumber
½ to 1 cup cubed honeydew
Pinch of sea salt

DIRECTIONS:

Wash your produce extremely well and cut into juice-able chunks. Process all ingredients through the juicer. Make sure to scrape off the foam that forms on top of the juice before drinking. Serve with a pinch of salt before drinking.

Everything but the Bitchin' Sink

DID YA KNOW?

Green juice is packed with chlorophyll, which helps the bod detox and improves oxygen circulation. It also balances your body's pH by reducing acidity.

Also known as, "fridge cleaner." This savory juice is another amazing lunch/dinner option that can double as a soup. Cayenne pepper does wonders for your stomach and intestinal tract, while also providing antioxidants, vitamins B$_6$ and E, potassium, and manganese.

INGREDIENTS:

2 leaves kale
1 stalk celery
1 carrot
⅕ yellow pepper
1" piece of fresh ginger root
1" piece of red onion, peeled
1 lemon, peeled
1 clove garlic, peeled
1 pinch cayenne pepper

DIRECTIONS:

Wash all produce. Remove the seeds and white membrane from the bell pepper. Cut all produce into juice-able chunks. Process all produce through juicer and serve with a pinch of cayenne pepper.

Hang Out with Your Cuke Out

Pears are an understated but amazing fruit, filled with vitamins B_2, C, and E, copper, and potassium. Fresh mint gives this juice a deliciously refreshing flavor, while doing you some good: it promotes healthy digestion and soothes stomach irritation (drink mint tea/juices when your stomach is acting up). This juice may seem like a strange breakfast option, but the mint is so revitalizing and wakes you up like a cup of coffee never could!

INGREDIENTS:

2 cucumbers
2 limes, peeled
2 pears
1 handful of fresh mint,
plus extra for garnish
1 heaping handful of watercress

DIRECTIONS:

Wash all produce well and prep into juice-able chunks. Process ingredients through juicer and garnish your cup with an extra mint sprig because you deserve some extra freshness in your life.

better
THAN
V8
(but who's counting?)

This fresh powerhouse of fruits and veg is the Bloody Mary 2.0; you're guaranteed a merry time, always. A little parsley goes a long way here as it's an amazing source of vitamins A, C, and K, and it has strong antioxidant and anti-inflammatory properties. The carrots add a healthy sweetness that keep you drinking, while the greens keep you going.

INGREDIENTS:

3 carrots
3 large stalks celery
½ cucumber
1 red pepper
Handful of parsley
1 lemon
1 lime
4 tomatoes
1" chunk of fresh ginger
Pinch of sea salt
Pinch of cayenne pepper
3 drops oregano oil
1 stalk celery, for garnish

DIRECTIONS:

Wash all produce well. Cut all ingredients into juice-able pieces. Juice and serve with the celery stalk, à la Bloody Mary (but much better for you).

Do You Play
Squash?

1 SERVING — LEVEL III, LG, SB, AI

Now you do! Summer squash is one of the top food sources for beta-carotene and alpha-carotene, in addition to having high amounts of antioxidants and vitamin C. Meaning this guy is anti-inflammatory and can aid in cancer prevention. Guess who just became your favorite vegetable?

INGREDIENTS:

½ cucumber
1 summer squash
½ fennel bulb
1 apple
Handful of parsley
1" piece of fresh ginger
1 lime

DIRECTIONS:

Wash all produce well and prepare into juice-able chunks. Make sure to core the apple and peel the lime. Process through the juicer and serve.

Fat Burning 101

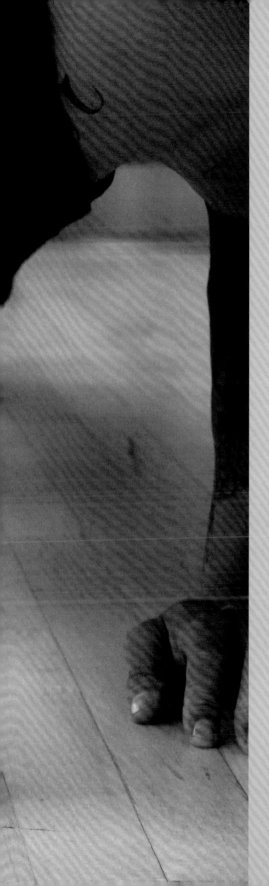

If you're still green to juicing, allow me to veg-ucate you. Cabbage has an extremely low calorie content, but a crazy-impressive assortment of nutrients. It's rich in antioxidants and phytonutrients, which help boost your defense mechanisms against cancer, and it aids in detoxification against harmful toxins and hormones. So next time someone calls you a cabbage patch kid, be like, THANK YOU. Class dismissed.

INGREDIENTS:

½ head green cabbage
½ cucumber
1 bunch of dandelion greens
½ lemon
1" chunk of fresh ginger root

DIRECTIONS:

Wash all produce well and cut all ingredients into juice-able pieces. Juice and enjoy.

Fountain of Youth

1 SERVING — LEVEL III, LG, SB, AI

You can stop now because you've found the secret to looking and feeling hella youthful. Cucumber is extremely hydrating and has amazing skin benefits. It refreshes your skin and its high amount of vitamin C helps build collagen and elastin, giving your skin that oomph that no lotion can pull off.

INGREDIENTS:

1 cucumber
Handful of parsley
1 yellow bell pepper
Handful of basil
½ lemon, peeled
½ tsp to 1 tbsp spirulina (optional, see note)

DIRECTIONS:

Wash all produce. Remove the seeds and white membrane from the bell pepper. Cut all produce into juice-able chunks. Process through the juicer and serve.

TIP:

I love adding spirulina to this juice. You can add it to any juice, but the rich blue-green algae complements this recipe nicely. Just add ½ tsp to 1 tbsp (depending on how much you can handle the truth) and mix it in with a spoon.

Not So Green Machine

2 SERVINGS — LEVEL III, LG, SB, AI

This veg powerhouse is a deliciously savory juice, ideal for hearty snacking or lunch/dinner. While most people either love or hate cilantro, everyone should bow down to this wondrous herb. It's filled with antioxidants, essential oils, and vitamins that can help regulate bad cholesterol levels. If you're feeling extra virtuous, add on some olive oil for heart-healthy fat.

INGREDIENTS:

1 large tomato
2 large celery stalks
1 carrot
½ cucumber
Large handful of cilantro
1 to 2 tsp extra virgin olive oil (optional)

DIRECTIONS:

Wash all produce well and cut into juice-appropriate pieces. Process through the juicer and serve, adding the olive oil right before drinking (if using).

The Sagacious Sage

1 SERVING — LEVEL III, LG, AI, SB

Want some sage advice? Eat more of it . . . sage, that is. Sage is incredibly antioxidant and anti-inflammatory. It's recommended for people with conditions like arthritis and asthma. Sage is also said to boost your ability to remember things. Pretty fitting, huh?

INGREDIENTS:

½ lemon, peeled
1 small handful of sage
1 cucumber
1 pear
1 bunch of kale

DIRECTIONS:

Wash all produce and cut into juice-able chunks. Run through the juicer and serve.

Get Green-ish

1 SERVING — LEVEL III, LG, SB, AI

It's no wonder Popeye was such a hunk-a-lunk. This juice has spinach at its rawest and most beneficial to your bod. Packed with antioxidants, folate, protein, fiber, iron, and practically an alphabet of vitamins, this powerhouse of good helps to lower high blood pressure and maintains brain sharpness.

INGREDIENTS:

1 bunch of spinach
2 carrots
½ lemon
1 apple

DIRECTIONS:

Wash all produce well. Core the apple, and cut all ingredients into juice-able pieces. Juice and enjoy.

Green Goddess

2 SERVINGS — LEVEL III, LG, AI, SB

This incredible combo of greens will unleash your inner goddess, and if you already embrace your goddess-ness, then get ready to embrace your green goddess-ness. This juice is one of my faves; it's packed with health-goods with a hint of apple sweetness. It doesn't hurt that it's rich in calcium, copper, iron, potassium, and vitamins B_1, B_2, C, E, and K.

INGREDIENTS:

5 to 6 leaves kale
2 large handfuls of spinach
1 green apple
½ cucumber
4 to 6 celery stalks
3 to 4 sprigs fresh mint
Handful of parsley
Handful of cilantro

DIRECTIONS:

Wash all produce well. Core the apple and cut all ingredients into juice-able pieces. Juice and enjoy.

You're Welcome, Liver

1 SERVING — LEVEL III, LG, AI

This antioxidant powerhouse is meant to give your liver a well-deserved break so it can get to cleansing out toxins. Carrot juice is highly alkalizing, helping your liver further detox. Ginger adds a fiery, sweet taste to mask any overly cabbage taste.

INGREDIENTS:

1 celery stalk
½ cucumber
2 carrots
¼ cup red cabbage
1" chunk of fresh ginger root
Handful of parsley

DIRECTIONS:

Wash all produce well. Cut all ingredients into juice-able pieces. Juice and enjoy.

Kale the Pain Away

1-2 SERVINGS — LEVEL III, LG, SB, AI

You should always suck/eat celery 'cause it's known to lower blood pressure and prevents the degeneration of vision, so you'll be looking real good and seeing even better. This beast of a juice kales the toxins away—KALE YEAH! It has tons of protein, folate, alpha-lonolenic acids, and vitamins A, C, and K to make ya say, "ACK, this is so good!"

INGREDIENTS:

2 tomatoes
1 bunch of Swiss chard leaves
1 bunch of kale leaves
1 bunch of spinach leaves
½ head romaine lettuce
2 celery stalks
½ cucumber
1 garlic clove, peeled
Handful of fresh basil leaves
Extra virgin olive oil (optional)
Black pepper (optional)

DIRECTIONS:

Wash all produce well and prep into juice-able chunks. Send everything through your juicer and serve with a drizzle of olive oil and a sprinkle of black pepper. Yum!

Asparagus-ade

No jokes about stinky asparagus pee here, only benefits. Asparagus is packed with folate and vitamins A, C, E, and K. Not only is asparagus incredibly antioxidant and said to prevent cancer, it can also help in regulating your blood pressure, thanks to its abundant source of vitamin B.

INGREDIENTS:

1 cucumber
3 kale leaves
10 asparagus spears
1 lemon, peeled

DIRECTIONS:

Wash all produce and cut into juice-able chunks. Process through your juicer and serve.

Green Revolution

1 SERVING — LEVEL III, LG, AI, SB

Swiss chard takes the cake for being a babe-inducing veg. Wait, are you thinking about cake now? Stop that. Thanks to your new leafy green friend, this juice is far sexier for your insides and outsides. It contains a bundle of vitamins—including A, B_2, B_6, C, E, and K—as well as iron, fiber, beta-carotene, zinc, folate, calcium, biotin, and . . . okay, I'm tired now. Just drink it for mad detoxification and shedding of those unwanted pounds!

INGREDIENTS:

1 bunch of swiss chard, leaves only
4 celery stalks
2 carrots
1 red bell pepper
1 lemon, peeled
1" piece of ginger

DIRECTIONS:

Wash all produce well. Cut all ingredients into juice-able pieces. Juice and enjoy.

[FRUITY JUICES]

Juices that are tasty and fruity, but still serious business. We're not messin' around here. These recipes have lots of fresh, seasonal fruit that you should buy as local as possible for ultimate satisfaction. There are hints of veg, but these juices mainly highlight the amazing rainbow of fruit.

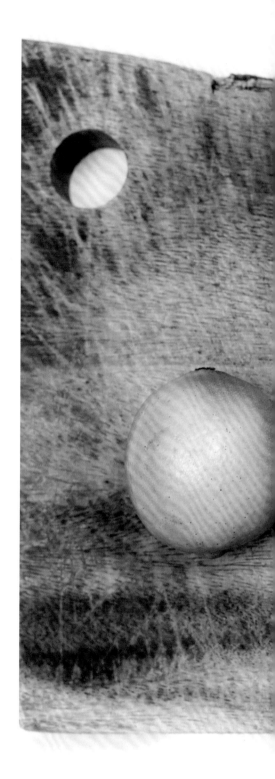

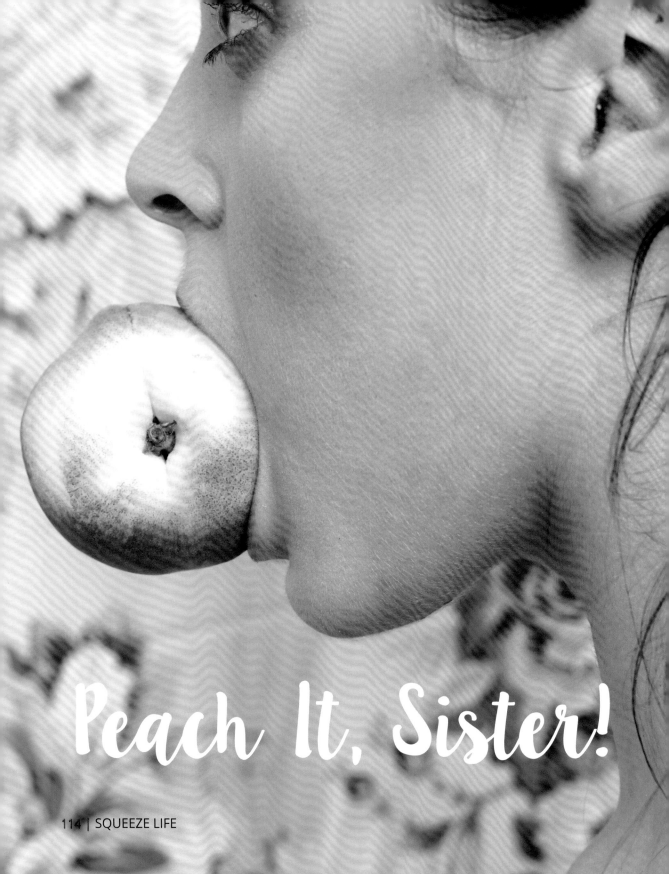

Peach It, Sister!

DID YA KNOW?

Peaches provide 15 percent of your daily vitamin C needs. They're also abundant in vitamins E and K, niacin, folate, iron, potassium, magnesium, phosphorus, zinc, and copper. How peachy!

1 SERVING — LEVEL II, AI, SB

Peaches rawk the world. You never hear a song about strawberries or a football game named after a grape. Suckers! Just kidding strawberries and grapes, we love you too. Don't refrigerate peaches! They taste so much better when they're warm and ripe, fresh from the farm.

INGREDIENTS:

1 cucumber
1 peach
Small handful of leafy greens, chef's choice
Small handful of fresh mint
¼" chunk of fresh ginger root
¼ cup pineapple chunks

DIRECTIONS:

Wash all your produce well. Cut, core, and quarter the peach. Prep all produce so it seamlessly fits through your juicer. Juice away and serve.

I **really** LOVE *your* PEACHES

1 SERVING — LEVEL II, SB, AI

This deliciously spiced juice is the perfect breakfast or snack! The cinnamon and clove powders add delicious flava, and the peaches and pear make this just sweet enough. Cinnamon (in small doses) can lower blood sugar levels and reduce heart disease, and it's a powerful antioxidant. Cloves are useful in detoxifying and are actually quite nutrient-dense (vitamin K, iron, magnesium, and calcium).

INGREDIENTS:

2 peaches
1 Asian pear
2 celery stalks
1" chunk of fresh ginger root
Pinch of cinnamon
Pinch of clove powder

DIRECTIONS:

Wash all produce well and cut into juice-able pieces. Run all produce through the juicer and sprinkle on the cinnamon and clove before serving. Enjoy!

Sherbet Lemonade

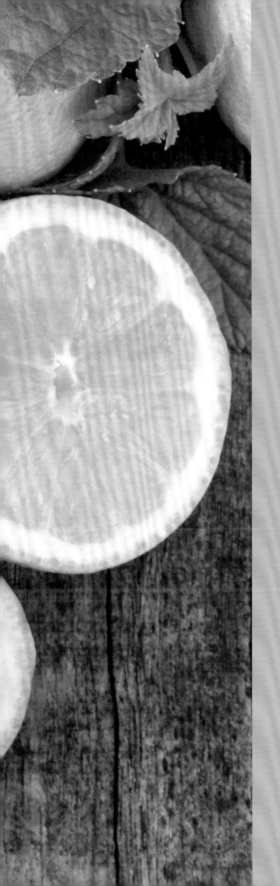

1 SERVING — LEVEL II, SB, AI

This is the simplest and quite possibly tastiest juice you'll ever make. If you forgot to stock your veg arsenal, you'll most likely still be able to make this. The sweetness of the apples slightly offsets the tangy lemon, making this the best goddamn lemonade ever. Or shall we say, lemon-AID? It's packed with antioxidants, vitamins A, B, and C, and it kick-starts the detoxifying process (especially in the liver and kidneys). We're not kidney, this is the good stuff.

INGREDIENTS:

3 apples
1 yellow pepper
1½ lemons

DIRECTIONS:

Wash all produce well. Core the apples and cut all ingredients into juice-able pieces. Juice and enjoy.

Peachy Clean, Jellybean!

2 SERVINGS — LEVEL II, AI

It may seem weird to juice a sweet potato but believe me, it's so delicious and creamy! This sweet juice is the perfect blend of sweet potatoes, peaches, and pears. The sweet potatoes add a rich creaminess to the juice, but they're also an excellent source of vitamins A and C, manganese, and copper.

INGREDIENTS:

2 sweet potatoes
3 peaches, pitted
2 pears, cored
1" chunk of fresh turmeric root (or substitute 1 tsp dried turmeric powder)
1" chunk of fresh ginger root
Pinch of cinnamon

DIRECTIONS:

Wash all produce and prep into juice-able chunks. Process through juicer, serve, and sprinkle some cinnamon on top.

VACAY
state
OF
mind

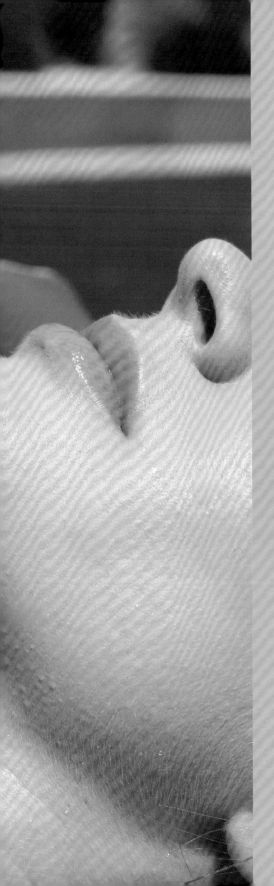

2 SERVINGS — LEVEL I, SB, AI

This juice is a practically a tropical vacation in a glass. Yes, you're welcome. Pineapples are rumored to have some interesting powers when ingested by men . . . while I won't get into that, I'll say that pineapples are incredibly rich in vitamin C and antioxidants. Pineapples also have a good amount of vitamin B that works as a factor in providing energy!

INGREDIENTS:

4 carrots
1 apple
1 orange
1½ cups pineapple chunks
Handful of fresh mint leaves
1 cucumber

DIRECTIONS:

Wash all produce well. Core the apple and cut all ingredients into juice-able pieces. Juice and enjoy.

Pucker Up!

DID YA KNOW? An easy way to separate pomegranate seeds: simply cut the pom in half and submerge in a bowl of water. Then separate the seeds from the membrane underwater (that way you avoid any juice spritz that can stain your clothes). The membrane will float, while the seeds sink. DONE!

3 SERVINGS — LEVEL II, SB, AI

There's nothing better than a set of melons . . . watermelons, that is. This juice is round and juicy! It's intensely sweet and sour. But don't be put off, it is amazingly delicious and refreshing! Pomegranates are one of the densest fruits of all time. They support your immune system and help lower cholesterol. Watermelons are also aphrodisiacs, so you're going to want to schedule some time with your babe upon drinking this.

INGREDIENTS:

2 pomegranates
2 cups watermelon
½ cucumber
1 ruby grapefruit
1 lime
1 small red chili pepper

DIRECTIONS:

Wash all produce well. Peel and remove the seeds from the pomegranates. Cut other produce into juice-able chunks and process through the juicer. Enjoy!

squeeze this

DID YA KNOW?

Cranberries BOUNCE! Seriously, try it for yourself. This wonder fruit contains air pockets, which allow them to float and bounce. Most fun berry ever.

2 SERVINGS — LEVEL II, SB, AI

Yer going to want to squeeze this to the last drop, it's so good! Aloe is incredibly soothing, anti-inflammatory, and it does wonders for your skin and hair. The cranberries and pears add a nice sweetness to this juice for sweet, sweet drinkability.

INGREDIENTS:

2 cups cranberries, fresh or frozen
(make sure to thaw frozen cranberries)
2 pears
2 tbsp aloe vera juice
1 lime

DIRECTIONS:

Wash all produce. Cut the pears and lime into juice-able pieces. Juice all ingredients and serve.

I Have a Heart-On

2 SERVING — LEVEL II, AI, SB

Blueberries are a wonder fruit! These blue balls are *packed* with antioxidant properties, but what may be most remarkable is that they are incredibly beneficial for cardiovascular health. They lower bad cholesterol levels and raise antioxidant capacity in the bloodstream, meaning the intake of antioxidants will be even more powerful!

INGREDIENTS:

2 cups fresh blueberries
2 cups fresh spinach leaves
2 apples
½ cup canteloupe

DIRECTIONS:

Wash all produce well and core your apples. Juice all ingredients and enjoy!

Strawberry Lemonade

2 SERVINGS — LEVEL II, SB, AI

This isn't your momma's strawberry lemonade. The addition of jicama adds an insane amount of antioxidants and vitamin C, which makes this juice great for fighting inflammations, coughs, and colds.

INGREDIENTS:

12 strawberries, hulled
3 lemons, peeled
1 apple
3 parsnips
2 cups jicama

DIRECTIONS:

Wash all produce well. Core the apples and cut all produce into juice-able pieces. Run all ingredients through the juicer and serve.

Looking Good
is the Sweetest
Revenge

1 SERVING — LEVEL II, SB

Let's be real: when you feel good, you look good. This juice will make you feel GOOD. Like, damn I feel so fine right now. Packed with vitamin C, potassium, folic acid, and antioxidant properties, you might as well call this one the "I'm the shit" juice.

INGREDIENTS:

3 apricots
1 orange, peeled
1 lemon
3 carrots
1 fennel bulb

DIRECTIONS:

Wash all produce well. Cut all ingredients into juice-able pieces. Juice and feel the antioxidants do good stuff to your body. Feel free to wink at innocent bystanders.

Citrus Daze

DID YA KNOW? You can use your own aloe plant to get aloe juice! Simply fillet the leaf and separate its gelatinous interior from the skin, then run the gelatinous part through the juicer. If you juice the whole thing with its skin still on, it'll be bitter. If you don't have access to an aloe plant, you can use high-quality store-bought aloe vera juice in the recipes that call for it.

1-2 SERVINGS — LEVEL II, SB

Arguably the best kind of daze to be in! This juice is incredibly packed with vitamin C. I recommend getting a load of it when you're not feeling your best, it'll perk ya right back up. Aloe vera is amazing for your hair, but it's also great for settling digestion, lowering cholesterol, and boosting your mineral intake. The pineapple is optional in this recipe, so go for it if you want that extra sweetness.

INGREDIENTS:

2 navel oranges, peeled
1 grapefruit, peeled
¼ cup aloe vera juice
½ cup pineapple chunks (optional)

DIRECTIONS:

Wash all produce well. Make sure your oranges and grapefruit are peeled and quarter them. Juice all produce and combine with the aloe vera juice. Serve.

Popeye Lemonade

2 SERVINGS — LEVEL II, SB, LG

We already know that Popeye was definitely on to something with spinach. This leafy green is loaded with iron, protein, and vitamins that are crucial for good skin and bone health. The apples and pear are great in disguising the spinach taste, if you haven't learned to love it yet.

INGREDIENTS:

4 bunches of spinach
2 lemons, peeled
1 cucumber
1 pear
1 Granny Smith apple

DIRECTIONS:

Wash all produce well. Core and slice the apples and pear. Juice all ingredients and drink!

Juicy Melons

2 SERVINGS — LEVEL 1 , SB

Watermelons are mostly water—duh—but they're insanely nutritious and will make ya real bootylicious. They have high levels of vitamins A, B_6, and C, and antioxidants, but the rind actually has some sexy benefits. It contains L-citrulline, which boasts libido-boosting powers, so you can make real good use of those juicy melons.

INGREDIENTS:

4 cups watermelon, with a bit of its rind
1 lime

DIRECTIONS:

Wash all produce well and cut into juice-able chunks. Process through the juicer and enjoy.

[COMBO JUICES]

These recipes are the mature Goldilocks of the juice world: not too green, not too sweet, but always hella sexy. They're a happy medium between straight up green juice and fruity tootys. Great for breakfast, lunch, dinner, snaxxx, anytime really.

NOT your MOMMA'S beauty SECRET

3 SERVINGS — LEVEL II, SB, AI

There are certain rituals you should get into the habit of everyday: drinking tons of water, checking your fine-ass self out in the mirror, and drinking this elixir. I'm very into this juice because it's not only packed with a variety of veggies, but it's also quite customizable. Pick whatever leafy greens you happen to have stocked—any color beets, some red peppers, and you're good to go.

INGREDIENTS:

1 large handful of greens
1 cup cabbage
1 Granny Smith apple
4 stalks celery
4 carrots
3 red or golden beets, or a combo
1 large cucumber
1 lemon
1 lime
2 bell peppers, either red, yellow, or orange
2" chunk of fresh ginger

DIRECTIONS:

Wash all produce well. Core the apple and cut all ingredients into juice-able pieces. Juice and enjoy!

Flower Power

1 SERVING — LEVEL II, SB, AI

This juice is so unique! It tastes very woodsy and earthy, even though it looks just like a plain ole green juice. The addition of burdock adds to this phenomenal taste. Burdock is a type of root that comes from a really beautiful plant. But not only is burdock beautiful, it's a potent detoxifier! This powerful root is a great source of polysaccharides that support the liver and release toxins from the blood. This juice is perfect for targeting bacterial infections and for getting rid of any inflammatory skin conditions.

INGREDIENTS:

3" piece of burdock root
1" chunk of fresh ginger
2 green apples
1 bunch of kale leaves
1 lemon

DIRECTIONS:

Wash all produce well and cut into juice-able pieces. Process through your juicer and serve.

Itsy Bitsy Tiny Weeny Yellow Polka Dot Juice-ini

1 SERVING — LEVEL II, AI

This juice will definitely help you get into that itsy bitsy yellow polka dot bikini (and maybe even out of it!). Rutabagas are incredibly helpful in improving your metabolic functions. The slight sweetness of the bell pepper and apple pairs perfectly with the rutabaga to create a kickass juice.

INGREDIENTS:

2 yellow bell peppers, with the stems and seeds removed
1 rutabaga, peeled
1 golden delicious apple, cored
1 pear
1 lemon, peeled
1½" chunk of fresh ginger, skin removed

DIRECTIONS:

Wash all produce well and cut into juice-able pieces. Run all produce through the juicer and serve.

Plum Her?

I Hardly Know Her!

1 SERVING — LEVEL II, AI, SB

This vibrant juice is rich with antioxidants and anthocyanin compounds, which have been found to be anti-inflammatory, cancer preventative, and helpful in preventing cardiovascular disease, obesity, and diabetes.

INGREDIENTS:

2 plums

1 pint fresh blueberries 1 pint fresh blueberries (or whatev berries ya got in the fridge)

1" chunk of fresh ginger

½ head romaine

1 apple, cored

½ tsp cinnamon

DIRECTIONS:

Wash all produce well. Pit the plums and slice everything into juice-able pieces. Run produce through the juicer and stir in the cinnamon before serving.

Godzilla Fuel

2 SERVINGS — LEVEL II, AI, SB

I think that Godzilla was a misunderstood creature. Maybe he was going through some personal issues, or maybe he just really needed a rainbow juice to balance him out. Can you imagine the clogged colon on that guy (ew, don't)? This juice would've probably chilled him out, but it can certainly still turn you around. It's a little sweet, very delicious, and has a bit of everything you need to kick-start your health.

INGREDIENTS:

1 handful of spinach
1 lime, peeled
3 oranges
½ cup blueberries
½ cucumber
4 carrots
1 beet
1 celery stalk

DIRECTIONS:

Wash all produce well. Prep all ingredients into juice-able pieces. Juice and enjoy.

Fab Fennel

1-2 SERVINGS — LEVEL II, AI, SB

This sweet juice has lots of undercover greens for extreme drinkability and maximum nutrient satisfaction. Licorice-delish fennel contains vitamin C, potassium, and a high concentration of folic acid, which is necessary for healthy DNA replication. This juice may or may not also lead to human replication . . . if you catch my drift.

INGREDIENTS:

1 fennel bulb

2 Granny Smith apples

2 handfuls of spinach, or any other leafy green you like

1 pear (Bartlett pears work nicely here)

1 mango

1 celery stalk

1" chunk of fresh ginger

DIRECTIONS:

Wash all produce well. Core the apples and pear, and cut all ingredients into juice-able pieces. Juice and enjoy.

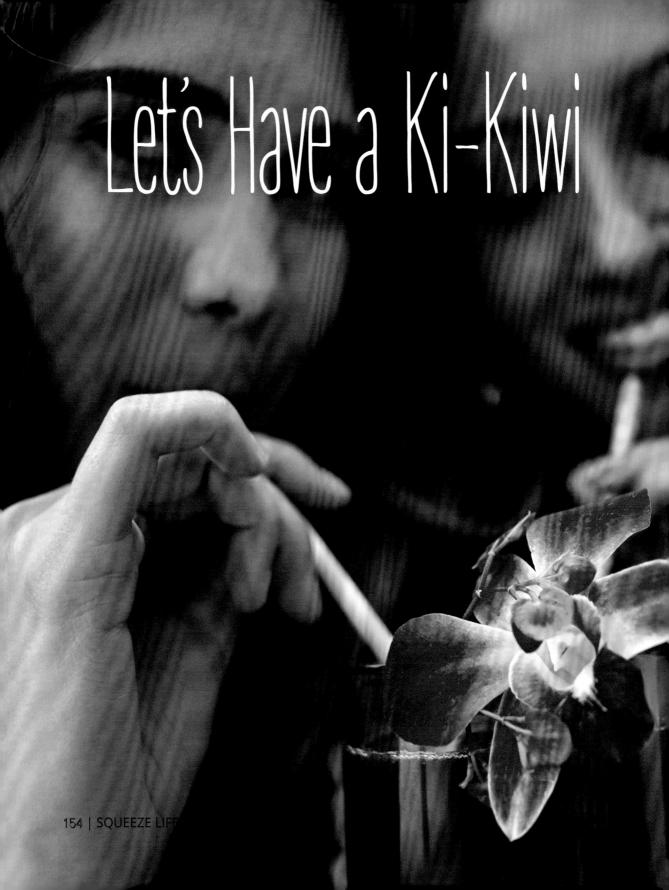

Let's Have a Ki-Kiwi

This juice is sweet and tangy, and super refreshing! Kiwis are high in vitamin C and awesome for aiding in digestion. They're also energizing, help cleanse respiratory issues, and contain chlorophyll (which can curb hunger cravings).

INGREDIENTS:

2 kiwis
1 cucumber
1 cup raspberries
1 apple
½ lemon, peeled

DIRECTIONS:

Wash all ingredients well and cut into juice-able pieces. Process everything through a juicer and serve.

Juice Life

1 SERVING — LEVEL I, SB, AI

Jicama is rich with vitamins A, C, K, and B, and it also contains sodium and potassium, which are both essential in alkalizing the blood. Additionally, jicama is an antioxidant and helps your hot bod fight infections. Try shredding jicama and eating it as a raw salad too!

INGREDIENTS:

¼ cup purple cabbage

1 apple

3 carrots

1½ cups jicama

1" chunk of fresh ginger

DIRECTIONS:

Wash all produce well. Core the apple and cut all ingredients into juice-able pieces. Juice and enjoy.

Orange You Glad It's Butternut Squash?

1 SERVING — LEVEL II, SB

Butternut squash's color is actually a great indication of its health benefits. The orange hue indicates that the veg is filled with carotenoids (said to fight heart disease) and beta-carotene (an antioxidant that your bod transforms into vitamin A). Butternut squash and carrots are an orange combo that makes this juice sweet, creamy, and your source for healthy skin and eyes.

INGREDIENTS:

2 carrots
1 cup butternut squash, cubed
1 red bell pepper
½ head romaine lettuce

DIRECTIONS:

Wash all produce and cut into juice-able pieces. Process all ingredients through the juicer and serve.

Sweet Green Lick-orice

1 SERVING — LEVEL II, AI, SB

This green juice is sweetened by the refreshing cantaloupe and the licorice-tasting fennel, which also adds immune-boosting capabilities from its abundant amounts of vitamin C. Fennel is also said to be cancer preventative.

INGREDIENTS:

3 kale leaves
7 asparagus spears
½ head fennel
½ cantaloupe

DIRECTIONS:

Wash all produce well and cut into juice-able pieces. Run produce through the juicer and serve.

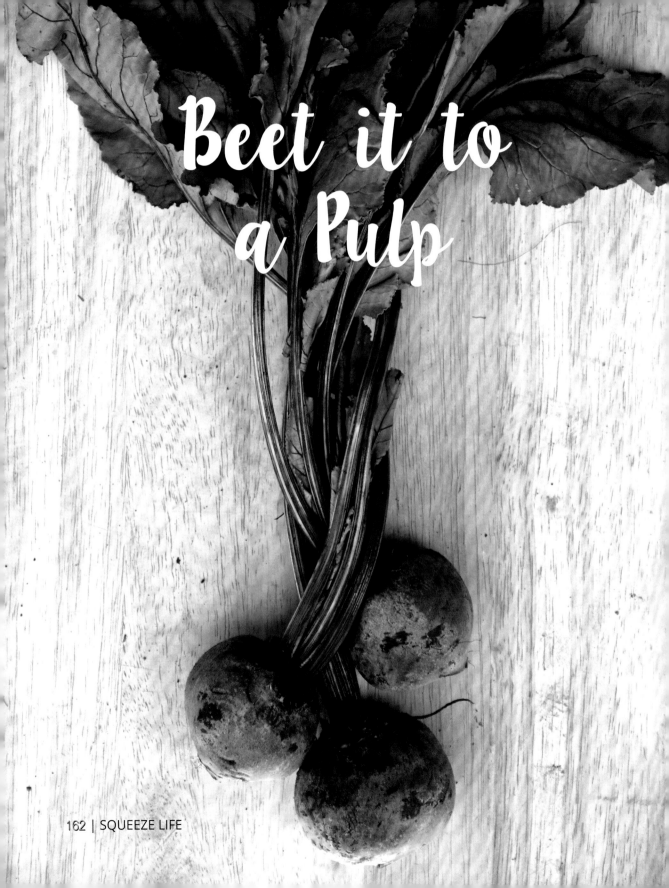

Beet it to a Pulp

DID YA KNOW? You can juice stuff like pineapple cores and broccoli stalks that you wouldn't normally eat. More nutrients for me!

1-2 SERVINGS — LEVEL II, SB, AI

The beet adds a lovely hue to this juice, as well as high amounts of vitamin C (which are immune-boosting), potassium, and manganese (which are good for your bones, liver, kidneys, and pancreas).

INGREDIENTS:

1 beet
1 carrot
½ cup pineapple chunks
1" chunk of fresh ginger
1 lemon, peeled
2 Granny Smith apples

DIRECTIONS:

Wash all produce well. Cut off the root from the beet and core the apples. Process all ingredients through a juicer and serve.

LEAN,
green,
SEXY
machine

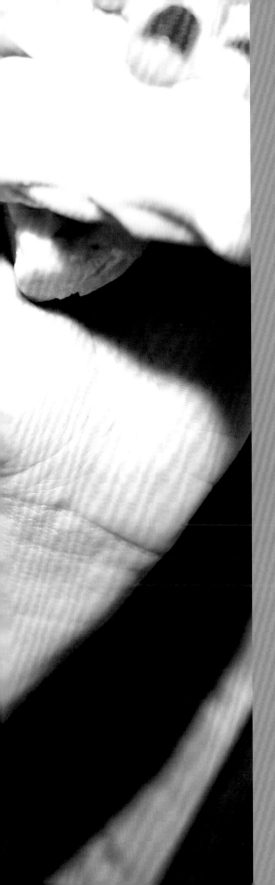

My favorite juices are the ones like this, simple and with an abundant amount of greens balanced with naturally sweet fruits. What else could you want? Broccoli has anti-inflammatory, antioxidant, and detox-supporting nutrients, making it a valuable ingredient for juicing whether you're on a cleanse or not.

INGREDIENTS:

1 head romaine lettuce
6 stalks celery
½ head broccoli
1 apple
1 mango
½ lemon

DIRECTIONS:

Wash all produce and cut into juice-able pieces. Run the produce through a juicer and serve.

Sweet
Potato Pie

1 SERVING — LEVEL II, SB, AI

This is Thanksgiving in a glass, but without the good ole tradition of stuffing yourself into a straight up food coma. This juice is definitely not coma-inducing, it'll actually perk ya up while satiating any pie cravings you may have! Sweet potatoes are an amazing ingredient to add in juices so they taste like dessert. They add a creaminess and sweetness that is unlike any sugar rush you'd have from a slice of pie.

INGREDIENTS:

2 carrots
2 sweet potatoes
1 red bell pepper
1 Fuji apple
½" chunk of fresh ginger root
Dash of cinnamon
Dash of nutmeg

DIRECTIONS:

Wash all produce and cut into juice-able pieces. Process through a juicer. Add cinnamon and nutmeg and serve.

[SPICY JUICES]

These juices help get ya blood pumping, your circulation flowing and your freak on! They usually include fiery ginger, radish, and/or some kind of pepper. Don't worry, though, they're perfectly balanced to not feel like you're guzzling down some hot sauce straight from the bottle. These are spicy and tasty (just like you, I bet).

Beet It Juice

2 SERVINGS — LEVEL II, SB, AI

This pretty juice is the ultimate cell-builder, thanks to your new friend, the beet. Beets will renew your hot bod with key minerals. Better yet, when combined with carrots, beets aid in kidney and liver function so your insides are as sexy as your outsides. *Me-ow*.

INGREDIENTS:

2 cucumbers
1 carrot
1 apple
1 beet
1" chunk of fresh ginger
1 cup pineapple chunks
¼ tsp cayenne pepper

DIRECTIONS:

Wash all produce well. Core the apple and cut all ingredients into juice-able pieces. Juice, top with cayenne pepper, and enjoy.

Spicy Pap-ay-a

1 SERVING — LEVEL II, AI

This juice is fiery, yet the papaya and strawberries add a sweet creaminess that's unbeatable. Cayenne pepper is great for kick-starting your metabolism and this juice will do just that! Papaya does wonders for your digestion and soothes stomach enzymes.

INGREDIENTS:

1½ cups papaya chunks
2 cups strawberries, hulled
2 navel oranges, peeled
½ lime, peeled
⅛ tsp cayenne pepper

DIRECTIONS:

Wash all produce well and cut into juice-able pieces. Juice and add cayenne prior to serving. Enjoy!

I'm Not Horsin' Around

DID YA KNOW?

Have a cold? Fresh horseradish root is your friend. Grate a little bit of horseradish (adjust to taste, this stuff is no joke) and make a tea with lemon and maple syrup. This should clear you right up.

You may be familiar with horseradish as a condiment, but it's actually a fresh root (sort of similar to ginger) that gives this juice a nice kick. Horseradish contains abundant levels of cancer-fighting compounds that aid in detoxifying any carcinogens. Oregano's essential oils are also incredibly antifungal and anti-inflammatory.

INGREDIENTS:

1 red pepper
1 tomato
1 lemon, peeled
1 cucumber
4 sprigs fresh oregano
1" chunk of fresh horseradish
Pinch of sea salt (optional)

DIRECTIONS:

Wash all produce well. Remove the stems, seeds, and white membrane from the red pepper. Prep all produce into juice-able chunks and process through the juicer. Serve and garnish with a pinch of sea salt, if using.

Garden Patch Kid

1-2 SERVINGS — LEVEL II, AI, SB, BH

This one's sweet, spicy, and tastes completely naughty . . . but *drumroll* it's not! So it tastes good and it's good for you? Yeah, I know . . . it'll take some getting used to. This is a good low-cal option that'll fill ya up with beta-carotene, vitamins A, B_1, B_2, B_6, and C. Spicy ginger will keep ya perky and warm, so drink it when you need a little boost.

INGREDIENTS:

1 beet

4 carrots

2 celery stalks

½ head cabbage, (purple cabbage gives this juice a great color)

Handful of flat leaf parsley

½ lemon, rind included

1" chunk of fresh ginger root

DIRECTIONS:

Wash all produce well and cut all ingredients into juice-able pieces. Juice and enjoy.

Get a Hold of These Melons

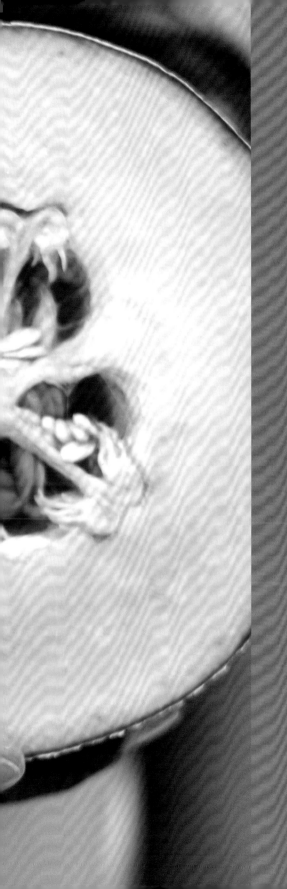

Juicy cantaloupe is a nutrient rainbow, with an array of vitamins to fill ya up. Dandelion greens are magical for your hot bod; they contain vitamins C and B_6, thiamin, riboflavin, calcium, iron, potassium, and manganese. Iron is crucial for generating blood cells, while potassium keeps ya heart healthy. Chug on!

INGREDIENTS:

½ cantaloupe

½ bunch of dandelion greens, or any other leafy greens you like

½ head broccoli

1 medium red chili pepper

DIRECTIONS:

Wash all produce well and cut into juice-able pieces. Juice and enjoy.

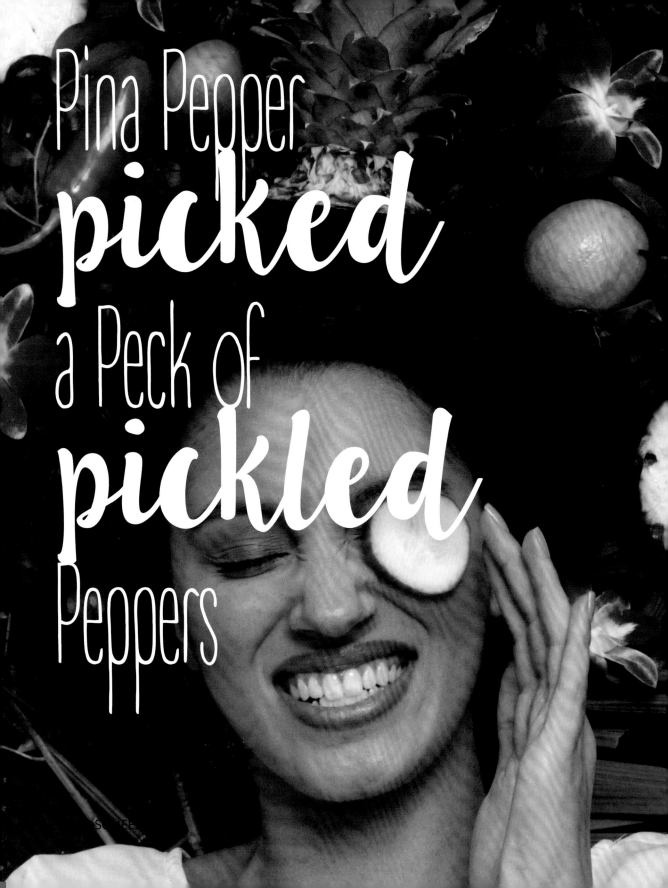

Pina Pepper **picked** a Peck of **pickled** Peppers

I can appreciate a good tongue twister when I see one (wink, wink). This combo of fruit, citrus, veg, and pepper is insanely rich with minerals, and chlorophyll and it'll hydrate you while some cutie appreciates you! Jalapeño adds a nice kick that'll warm up your system and improve circulation while boosting your metabolism. Not bad, not mad about it!

INGREDIENTS:

½ pineapple
1 cucumber
½ lime
½ jalapeño, seeded
1 orange
Handful of parsley

DIRECTIONS:

Wash all produce well and cut into juice-able chunks. Run through juicer and enjoy!

DID YA KNOW?

Pineapple is said to enhance the taste of semen, but I'll let you research that one.

The Detox
is Strong in
This One

1 SERVING — LEVEL III, LG, SB, AI

This juice's detox game is **strong**. The sweet tater and beet join forces to make this juice a beautiful hue, but most importantly, a delish treat filled with nutrients! It's packed with antioxidants, beta-carotene for your eyes, and vitamin A. Radishes do their diurectic thang and cleanse the hell out of your system by flushing everything out.

INGREDIENTS:

1 beet
1 large carrot
1 large parsnip
1 large celery stalk
½ sweet potato
1 cup radish

DIRECTIONS:

Wash all ingredients well. Peel the beet and cut everything into juice-able pieces. Juice and enjoy!

[TONICS, ELIXIRS, ETC.]

These recipes are like juice's party sister. They mainly have a juice base, but with added ingredients to make 'em really chill and refreshing. You'll find good-for-you sangria, mimosas, and spritzes in here so you can have a drink in one hand while you reeeeeelaxxx.

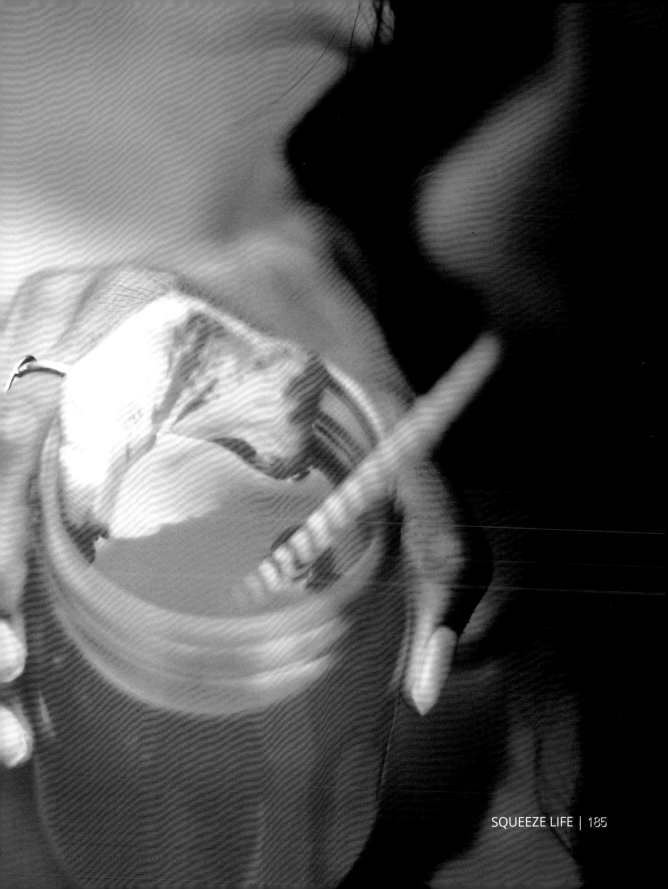

Funday Bloody Funday!

2 SERVINGS — LEVEL II, AI, NF

This is the perfect Sunday brunch drink, or really the perfect anytime drink, because it's so refreshing! Blood oranges contain tons of vitamin C (just like their traditional counterparts), but they're also a healthy source of anthocyanins, which are believed to be anti-inflammatory and help the body heal itself.

INGREDIENTS:

4 blood oranges
4 lemon basil sprigs
½ liter sparkling water

DIRECTIONS:

Wash all produce. Juice the oranges, then add the lemon basil and allow it to steep in the refrigerator for at least 3 hours. When ready to serve, strain, and top with the sparkling water. Enjoy!

CHOCOLATE

ginger

ELIXIR

This spicy, chocolatey elixir isn't for the faint of heart. It's sweet but still challenging to your palate. Not for beginners!

INGREDIENTS:

2 cups water

2 tbsp coconut oil

4 tbsp chia seeds (whole or, preferably, ground)

4 tbsp cacao powder

1½ tsp fresh ginger juice OR

1 tsp powdered ginger

Pinch of cayenne pepper

½ tsp vanilla extract OR vanilla powder

½ tsp cinnamon powder

3½ tbsp maple syrup

1 cup ice

Pinch of salt

DIRECTIONS:

Blend all ingredients together until smooth.

Hangover Cure

1 SERVING — LEVEL II, SB, NF

Here's to hoping that if you're hungover, you had a *really really* good time last night. This cure will get ya back and up at it! This citrus trio is a tasty way to rehydrate while providing you with all the nutrients and electrolytes you lost while you were partyin', ya naughty babe. Coconut mylk adds creaminess, protein, and a yogurt tang so you can feast on this the morning after when you can't stomach food. Better yet: drink this before you go to sleep to give your body a boost the next morning.

INGREDIENTS:

Juice of 1 lime
Juice of 1 lemon
1 grapefruit
1 cup coconut mylk (see recipe on page 218)
Pinch of sea salt

DIRECTIONS:

Wash all citrus well and cut into juice-able pieces. Process the citrus through the juicer, then mix with the coconut mylk. Add a pinch of salt before serving.

Butterfly Pea Tea Tonic

1 SERVING — LEVEL I , NF, AI, SB

Butterfly pea flowers are beautiful and make a delicious cup of blue-hued tea. It's similar to green tea, but earthy and woody. Mixed with the maple syrup and mylk, it creates a very refreshing beverage that's incredible for your immune system, healthy hair and skin, urinary probs, and detoxification, and it also stimulates blood circulation.

INGREDIENTS:

3 butterfly pea tea flowers
1 cup water
2 tbsp maple syrup
½ cup coconut mylk
Sparkling water

DIRECTIONS:

First, make the butterfly pea tea by mixing the flowers with water that is right off the boil. Steep for 10 minutes, then cool down. Mix well with the maple syrup and mylk then top off with sparkling water. Enjoy!

Sparkling Ginger-Aid

2-4 SERVINGS — LEVEL II, SB, AI, NF

Turmeric is all around awesome! It's known for being extremely anti-inflammatory and a great aid for headaches, menstrual cramps, and digestive issues (to name only a few!).

INGREDIENTS:

¼ cup fresh ginger juice

1 cup fresh apple juice

2 tbsp fresh lemon juice

2 tsp fresh turmeric OR
½ tsp powdered turmeric

3 to 5 tbsp maple syrup
OR coconut nectar

Sparkling water

DIRECTIONS:

Mix all ingredients, except the sparkling water, until well combined. Pour your mixture into your vessel of choice and top with sparkling water. I like to do half juice and half sparkling water, but you can play around with different proportions.

Sangria

Sure, red wine has some antioxidants, but nothing compares to the real deal. This sangria gives alcohol a run for its money and keeps ya hydrated with plenty o' vitamins.

INGREDIENTS:

2 beets

1 bunch of beetroot leaves (that are attached to your beets)

2 oranges

2 pears

2 cinnamon sticks

Pinch of cayenne pepper

3 tbsp maple syrup (optional, for sweetness)

2 cups any chopped fruit you like (apples, oranges, limes, pears, and melons are a good combo)

DIRECTIONS:

Wash all produce very well. Juice all produce, except the 2 cups of chopped fruit.

Add the juice along with the cinnamon, cayenne, and maple syrup to a large pitcher. Add the chopped fruit and marinate in the fridge for at least 30 minutes before serving.

My-mosa

2-4 SERVINGS — LEVEL I, AI, NF

This mimosa is still hella fancy, even without the champ added to it. Pineapple and ginger give this a tangy and spicy taste, while the sparkling water makes it poppin'! No cork needed.

INGREDIENTS:

1½ cups orange juice
½ cup pineapple juice
2 tbsp ginger juice
⅓ cup maple syrup OR coconut nectar
2 tbsp melted coconut butter
2 tbsp orange zest
Pinch of sea salt
2 cups sparkling water

DIRECTIONS:

Whisk all ingredients except sparkling water in a pitcher. Top off with 2 cups of sparkling water.

Skinny Spritz

Ahh, yes! Drink this spritz to refresh yo self and pretend you're a fancy-ass babe in Windsor Castle . . . or somewhere they serve spritzers! This tasty treat is a vitamin C boost that won't bum you out.

INGREDIENTS:

1 cup sparkling mineral water
2 cups grapefruit juice
½ lime, juiced
1 to 5 tbsp maple syrup, to taste
1 cup ice cubes
1/3 cup packed fresh basil leaves
Grapefruit rounds, for garnish

DIRECTIONS:

Mix all ingredients well, except for the ice cubes, basil, and grapefruit rounds. Add the basil leaves and pour the mixture over the ice. Garnish with grapefruit rounds. Drink right away or you can store in an airtight container for 1 hour to allow the basil to steep.

[MYLKS]

Dairy-free mylks, for the ultimate satisfaction, because if memory serves me right, mylk is comfort food. These recipes come with all the satiating nature of milk, minus the health risks.

Basic Almond Mylk

DID YA KNOW?

Humans are the only mammals that continue to drink milk after being weaned because we're sooo obsessed with getting enough calcium. All the while, plants provide all the calcium our bodies need without the health risks of milk. Dark leafy greens, broccoli, and almonds are some of the best non-dairy sources of calcium.

YIELDS 4 CUPS — LEVEL II

This mylk is anything but basic! It's a delicious and protein-packed base for so many recipes, but it's pretty tasty by itself too. Once you get the hang of it, feel free to play with different flavors: cinnamon, chai, vanilla, and even cocoa powder.

INGREDIENTS:

2 cups almonds
4 cups water
Pinch of sea salt

DIRECTIONS:

Blend everything until silky smooth. Strain through a nut milk bag or cheesecloth. Drink it up!

Fancy Almond Mylkyway

YIELDS 4 CUPS — LEVEL II, SB, AI

Like a candy bar but infinitely better for you! Say goodbye to your days of buying almond mylk at the store, especially when you have this treat by your side. Dates are nature's caramel, almonds are a healthy protein source, and coconut butter provides your dose of healthy fats.

INGREDIENTS:

1½ cups almonds

4 cups water

6 dates, pitted

1 tbsp coconut butter

½ tsp vanilla extract OR
1 vanilla bean, scraped

Pinch of sea salt

½ tsp cinnamon (optional)

DIRECTIONS:

Combine all ingredients in a blender until smooth. Strain the mixture through a nut milk bag or cheesecloth and chill thoroughly before drinking.

Sacha Inchi Mylk

YIELDS 2 CUPS — LEVEL II, SB, AI

You're probably thinking, **What the f*#@ is sacha inchi?** Okay, maybe you don't have a dirty mouth like I do, but the curiosity is still there! Sacha inchi is a plant that grows in the highlands of Peru, and it produces a seed that's very similar to a nut. It is extremely high in protein and contains a great amount of omega fatty acids. Use it like you would any other mylk!

INGREDIENTS:

1½ cups sacha inchi

2 cups water

2 tbsp maple syrup OR coconut nectar (optional, for added sweetness)

½ tsp vanilla extract OR 1 vanilla bean, scraped (optional)

1 tbsp sunflower lecithin, to emulsify

1 tbsp coconut butter OR coconut oil

DIRECTIONS:

Add all ingredients to a high-speed blender and process until smooth. Strain with a nut milk bag or cheesecloth. Keep in an airtight jar in the refrigerator for up to 2 days, maybe 3 if kept *very* cold.

Sunflower Seed Mylk

This one goes to all the babes that are allergic to nuts! This creamy sunflower seed mylk is a great source of vitamin E, meaning it's great for preventing cardiovascular disease.

INGREDIENTS:

1 cup raw sunflower seeds

3 cups water, or more to taste

½ tsp vanilla extract OR
1 vanilla bean, scraped

2 tbsp maple syrup OR 2 tbsp coconut nectar OR 6 pitted dates

1 tbsp sunflower lecithin (optional, for creaminess)

1 tbsp cocoa butter OR coconut oil (optional, for thickness)

Pinch of sea salt

DIRECTIONS:

Blend all ingredients together in a high-speed blender and strain through a nut milk bag or cheesecloth. Keep in an airtight jar in the refrigerator for 2 to 3 days.

Pumpkin Seed Mylk

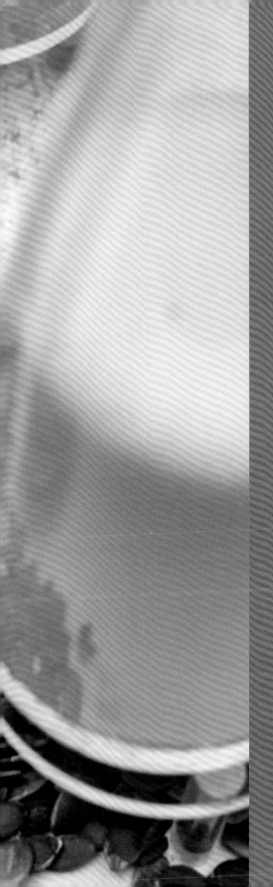

Another nut-free mylk option! Pumpkin seeds are packed with antioxidants and anti-microbial properties, they've been known to prevent diabetes, and they're great sources of vitamin E and zinc.

INGREDIENTS:

1 cup raw pumpkin seeds

3 cups water, or more to taste

½ tsp vanilla extract OR
1 vanilla bean, scraped

2 tbsp maple syrup OR 2 tbsp coconut nectar OR 6 pitted dates

1 tbsp sunflower lecithin (optional, for creaminess)

1 tbsp cocoa butter OR coconut oil (optional, for thickness)

Pinch of sea salt

DIRECTIONS:

Blend all ingredients together in a high-speed blender and strain through a nut milk bag or cheesecloth. Keep in an airtight jar in the refrigerator for 2 to 3 days.

Hemp mylk is an incredibly healthy choice for anyone seeking to improve digestion and metabolism, or to balance hormones. Their high amounts of omega-6 fatty acids help balance hormones. Hemp seeds also contain all twenty amino acids, including nine that our bodies simply can't produce!

HEMP SEED MYLK

INGREDIENTS:

1 cup raw hemp seeds, shelled

3 cups water, or more to taste

½ tsp vanilla extract OR
1 vanilla bean, scraped

2 tbsp maple syrup OR 2 tbsp coconut nectar OR 6 pitted dates

1 tbsp sunflower lecithin
(optional, for creaminess)

1 tbsp cocoa butter OR coconut oil (optional, for thickness)

Pinch of sea salt

DIRECTIONS:

Blend all ingredients together in a high-speed blender until smooth. Keep in an airtight jar in the refrigerator for 2 to 3 days.

Vanilla Coconut Mylk (Using Dried Coconut)

YIELDS 3½–4 CUPS
LEVEL I, LG, NF, SB

Similar benefits of the Coconut Mylk, without the machete.

INGREDIENTS:

1¾ cups shredded coconut OR raw unsweetened coconut chips, soaked at least 30 minutes

4 cups water

Pinch of sea salt

1 tsp vanilla extract OR

1 vanilla bean, scraped

3 dates, pitted (optional, for sweetness)

DIRECTIONS:

Add all ingredients to a high-speed blender and start by blending on low speed, slowly increasing to high speed. Blend for at least 2 minutes, or until the mylk is creamy and not chunky. Strain through a nut milk bag or cheesecloth. Keep coconut mylk in the fridge for up to a week.

CASHEW MYLK

YIELDS 3-4 CUPS — LEVEL 1

Cashews are one of the least fatty nuts, so drink away! They're known to prevent weight gain since they have healthy amounts of protein that curbs your appetite. This mylk is an amazing base for tons of smoothies and food recipes.

INGREDIENTS:

1 cup raw cashews

3 cups water

1 to 2 tbsp maple syrup
OR coconut nectar

½ tsp vanilla extract OR
1 vanilla bean, scraped

2 pinches of sea salt

DIRECTIONS:

If you don't have a super powerful blender, then it's best to use soaked cashews for this recipe (soak for at least 30 minutes). Simply blend all ingredients and strain through a nut milk bag or cheesecloth. If you have a high-speed blender, simply blend raw cashews with the rest of the ingredients. You don't need to strain if using a powerful blender.

Coconut Mylk (Using Fresh Coconut)

YIELDS 2-3 CUPS (WILL VARY DEPENDING ON THE SIZE OF YOUR COCONUT) — LEVEL 1, SB, AI, NF

You lucky devil! Looks like you got your hands on some fresh coconut. Not only are coconuts incredibly hydrating, they're highly nutritious and rich in vitamins C, E, B_1, B_5, and B_6 and minerals such as iron, sodium, calcium, magnesium, and phosphorous. Feel free to add 1 teaspoon of vanilla extract for a sweeter taste.

INGREDIENTS:

1 young Thai coconut (you'll need both the water and meat)
½ cup water

DIRECTIONS:

To open the coconut, it's best to use a large knife to cut a hole at the base. The hole needs to be large enough for you to scoop out the meat. The meat should be about 1 cup. Blend the coconut meat, coconut water, and water together in a high-speed blender until completely mixed.

Hemp Whore-chata

1-2 SERVINGS — LEVEL II, NF, AI, SB

This mylk is rich, refreshing, and ideal on a hot summer's day. Best consumed while chillin' on a hammock. Speaking of (banana) hammocks, the wondrous hemp seeds are rumored to be an aphrodisiac due to their abundance in vitamin E (known as the sex vitamin, for boosting the sex drive).

INGREDIENTS:

¼ cup hemp seeds

1½ cups almond mylk (see page 204) OR water

2 tbsp maple syrup OR coconut nectar

1 tsp cinnamon powder

2 tsp lacuma powder

½ tsp lemon juice

Pinch of sea salt

½ tsp spirulina (optional)

2 tbsp coconut oil

DIRECTIONS:

Combine all of the ingredients, except for the coconut oil, in a high-speed blender until nice and smooth. Slowly drizzle in the coconut oil while the blender is going. Refrigerate until chilled, shake the shit out of it, and serve!

The Alkalarian's Green

mylk

This mylk combines the best of both worlds: insanely nutritious green juice and comforting almond mylk. Spinach and almonds make this baby a protein powerhouse. Very satisfying.

INGREDIENTS:

1 cucumber
2 celery stalks
3 large handfuls of spinach
Almond mylk

DIRECTIONS:

Process all ingredients through your juicer. Mix equal parts green juice and almond mylk and drink up!

SMOOTHIES & SHAKES

These are blended, not juiced. Still good.

Shake it up, ya'll.

[HEALTHY/MEGA PROTEIN/ MEAL REPLACING SMOOTHIES]

Oooof, these smoothies are the ultimate example of good for you and even better for your taste buds. They're hearty, healthful, and so delicious you won't miss a thang during a cleanse. They're also ideal for post-workout meals.

Pecan Pie

2 SERVINGS — LEVEL I , AI

I MEAN . . . need I say any more? Live every day like it's Thanksgiving.

INGREDIENTS:

1½ cups water
⅔ cup pecans
8 soaked dates, pitted
¼ tsp cinnamon
½ tsp allspice
2½ cups frozen bananas
⅔ apple, cored
½ cup ice
Pinch of sea salt

DIRECTIONS:

Blend all ingredients together until smooth.

snickers
BAR
protein
SHAKE

1 SERVING — LEVEL I, AI, SB

Hungry? Don't grab a Snickers because it's essentially processed shit. Sorry, I'm not sorry! Get your bod shakin' with this shake that's filling and healthy. Brown rice proteins are fantastic muscle recoverers and encourage protein building, so gulp on this post-workout.

INGREDIENTS:

1 small handful of kale, stems removed

1 cup almond mylk (see page 204) OR water

1 frozen banana

3 tbsp cacao powder

2 tbsp almond butter OR 3 tbsp if using water instead of almond mylk

5 dates, pitted

1 tbsp coconut butter (optional)

1 tbsp fermented brown rice protein powder

½ cup ice

DIRECTIONS:

Wash the kale well. Throw all ingredients into the blender and blend on high speed for about 1 minute, until smooth. Add ice and blend until combined.

stimulate me

1-2 SERVINGS — LEVEL I, AI, SB

This caffeinated smoothie will get ya going in all the best ways possible! Unlike the traditional cup o' joe, cold brew coffee has less acidity—around 70 percent less than its heated counterpart. Hemp seeds and flax add tons of exxxtra protein so this is your all-in-one b-fast, baby.

INGREDIENTS:

1¼ cups cold brew coffee (see page 234)
¼ cup cashews, soaked
¼ cup almond butter
1 tbsp coconut oil
6 to 8 pitted dates, soaked
1 tsp hemp seeds, ground
1 tbsp flaxseed oil
Handful of ice cubes

DIRECTIONS:

Blend all ingredients except the ice cubes until smooth and creamy. If your cashews and dates weren't soaked, then make sure to blend a little longer to smooth it out. Add the ice and blend until smooth.

HOW TO MAKE
COLD BREW COFFEE

4 CUPS

Cold brew coffee is not just hot coffee gone cold, that shit's gross. With cold brew, fresh coffee is steeped with water for a long period of time to make an intensely delicious drank that's less acidic than the reg type of hawt coffee.

INGREDIENTS:

¾ cup coffee beans
4 cups water

DIRECTIONS:

Grind the coffee beans very coarsely. You want it to resemble kosher salt.

Add your ground beans to a large container (with or without a lid). Gradually add the water in and stir to make sure all grounds are moistened. Either place a lid on the container or cover with a cheesecloth. Let stand for 12 hours at room temperature.

Once steeped, strain your coffee with a fine mesh sieve or cheese cloth (or both for the ultimate silky brew). You can store cold brew in an airtight container in the fridge for up to 2 weeks.

NOTE:

You can also make cold brew using a French press. Simply follow the same process using the press's plunger as a way to strain the coffee.

stimulate me harder

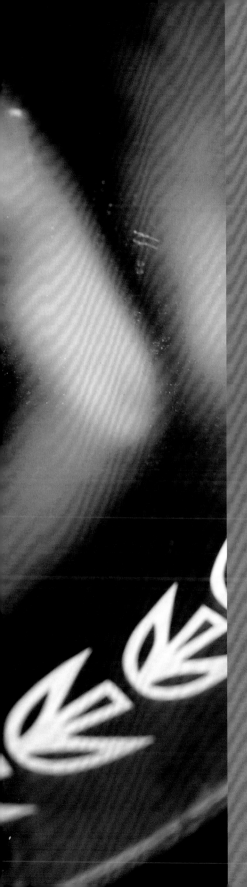

1-2 SERVINGS — LEVEL I, AI, SB

Don't worry, this decaf version is just as stimulating as the regular one. Maca is the sexxxcret ingredient here. It'll enhance your libido, and give ya a pump of energy and endurance so you can keep goin' all day, all night.

INGREDIENTS:

1¼ cups water
¼ cup cashews, soaked
¼ cup almond butter
2 tsp vanilla extract
1 tbsp coconut butter OR coconut oil
1 tbsp maca
Pinch of cinnamon
6 to 8 pitted dates, soaked
2 tsp hemp seeds, ground (optional)
1 tbsp flax seed oil (optional)
Handful of ice cubes

DIRECTIONS:

Blend all ingredients except the ice cubes until smooth and creamy. If your cashews and dates weren't soaked, then make sure to blend a little longer to smooth it out. Add the ice and blend until smooth.

blue-biotics

Adding coconut yogurt to smoothies will give a crazy boost of probiotics, which is a great digestive boost that'll keep your good bacteria balanced. Blueberries are sweet lil balls bursting with antioxidants that work to neutralize free radicals.

INGREDIENTS:

2 cups blueberries, fresh or frozen
½ cup coconut yogurt (see page 384)
1 frozen banana
2 to 4 pitted dates, soaked
(optional, for added sweetness)
Handful of ice, if not using frozen fruit

DIRECTIONS:

Blend all ingredients
together until smooth.

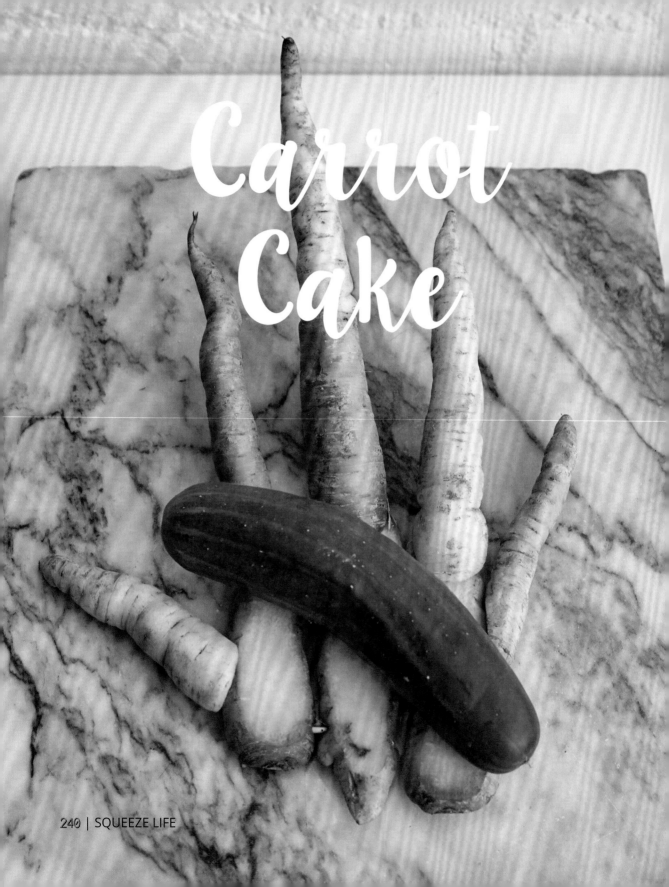

Carrot Cake

1-2 SERVINGS — LEVEL 1, AI, SB

This recipe is for times when people look at you, feeling all bad for you like you're missing out on all the deliciousness, when you say you are cleansing. Well, joke's on them, babe. Tastes like a giant slice of carrot cake the size of your face, but it's actually a hearty meal in a cup.

INGREDIENTS:

1 cup carrots, washed and chopped OR grated (if your blender isn't very powerful)
¼ cup cashews, soaked
2 tsp coconut oil
2 tbsp lemon juice
½" chunk of ginger, peeled, and minced OR ½ tsp ginger powder
½ tsp cinnamon powder
¼ tsp ground nutmeg
½ frozen banana
¼ cup dates, pitted
Pinch of sea salt
⅛ tsp ground cloves
Handful of ice
½ cup pineapple chunks (optional)

DIRECTIONS:

Blend all ingredients until silky smooth.

Banana Bread

2 SERVINGS — LEVEL 1, AI

This is one of my all-time fave smoothies! It's perfectly nutty, with hints of warm cinnamon and allspice. Forget about sad banana cereal for b-fast, gulp this down instead.

INGREDIENTS:

3 cups frozen bananas

½ cup walnuts

1 tsp vanilla

1 tsp cinnamon

⅛ tsp allspice

¼ tsp nutmeg

Pinch of sea salt

1 to 2½ cups water, depending on your desired thickness

1 tsp coconut oil

3 dates, pitted

1 cup ice (optional, depending on how frozen your bananas are)

DIRECTIONS:

Blend all ingredients together until smooth.

Vanilla Mint Chip Kiss

Yes, you can have this for lunch. I'm not kidding.

INGREDIENTS:

½ cup young coconut meat

¼ to ⅓ cup soaked dates, pitted

½ tsp vanilla extract OR
½ vanilla bean, scraped

¼ tsp mint extract OR a small
handful of fresh mint

2 tbsp coconut butter or coconut oil

1 cup mylk OR coconut water OR water

1 cup ice

2 tbsp cacao nibs

DIRECTIONS:

Blend everything, except for the cacao nibs, together until silky smooth. Top with cacao nibs and serve.

Apple Pie

1-2 SERVINGS — LEVEL I, AI

Now you can have your apple pie every day. You're welcome.

INGREDIENTS:

1 cup mylk (whatever your fave dairy-free option is)

2 apples, cored and chopped, with the skins on

1 tbsp hemp OR chia seeds

1 tsp vanilla extract

½ tsp ground cinnamon

¼ tsp nutmeg

Pinch of sea salt

4 dates, pitted

1 tbsp almond butter (optional)

½ cup ice cubes (optional)

DIRECTIONS:

Blend all ingredients until smooth.

Healthy Mint Chocolate Wish (Come True)

DID YA KNOW? You shouldn't and/or can't really juice: avocados (they don't really have juice), bananas (turn to mush that doesn't blend well with juice), or eggplants. Avos and bananas are excellent for blending in your fave smoothie.

2 SERVINGS — LEVEL 1, SB, AI

Chocolate and mint are a match made in heaven. Perhaps better than PB&J? Who knows? Who cares? This is a hearty as hell smoothie that tricks ya into thinking it's actually dessert.

INGREDIENTS:

1½ cups mylk (almond mylk works well in this recipe)

1 frozen banana

1 avocado

⅔ cup fresh spinach

8 mint leaves OR ⅛ tsp peppermint extract

4 soaked dates, pitted

¼ cup ice cubes

1 tbsp raw cacao nibs

DIRECTIONS:

Blend everything, except for the cacao nibs, together until silky smooth.
Top with cacao nibs and serve.

Double Chocolate Mint Bliss

Bliss, bliss, bliss! It's hard to call this a smoothie because it tastes more like a milkshake. Rich with protein and appropriately chocolaty, this one will go down so super easy that you'll be back for another glass ASAP.

INGREDIENTS:

1 frozen banana
¼ to ⅓ cup soaked dates, pitted
½ cup cocoa powder
1 cup coconut meat
1 cup water
¼ cup fresh mint leaves OR
½ tsp mint extract
1 tbsp maca
2 tbsp lacuma
1 tsp vanilla extract
Pinch of sea salt
2 handfuls of ice cubes
1 tbsp cacao nibs

DIRECTIONS:

Blend all ingredients, except for the cacao nibs, together until super smooth. Sprinkle cacao nibs on top and serve right away.

Almond Buttercup

You'll get used to drinking these almost too-good-to-be-true smoothies for meals (or hearty snacks), don't worry. It may seem hard at first, but drinking practically an almond cup in smoothie form is a piece of cake (and it almost tastes like it too). Flaxseed oil gives this recipe a healthy dose of heart healthy omega-3s that help fight inflammation.

INGREDIENTS:

2 frozen bananas
¼ cup cacao powder
2 tbsp almond butter
5 to 8 soaked dates, pitted
1 tbsp coconut oil
1 tsp flax oil (optional)
1 tsp hemp seeds (optional)
¼ tsp cinnamon
½ cup almond mylk OR water
Handful of ice cubes

DIRECTIONS:

Blend everything together until smooth.

Morning Delight

2 SERVINGS — LEVEL 1, NF

This hearty beverage will leave ya wanting more! Good news is that now you have the recipe and can make it whenever your heart desires. Coconut mylk adds a silky creaminess and the right amount of healthy fats so you'll feel satiated. Lacuma may seem like a weird sci-fi name, but it's actually a superfood hailing from Peru. It's low-glycemic and packed with antioxidants, fiber, and protein.

INGREDIENTS:

1½ cups coconut mylk (see recipe on page 218)
1 tsp lacuma
2 tsp pure matcha tea powder
2 frozen bananas
2 to 3 dates, pitted
1 tbsp maple syrup
½ tsp vanilla extract OR 1 vanilla bean
Small handful of ice (optional, depending whether you froze your nanners)

DIRECTIONS:

Add the coconut mylk, lacuma, and matcha to your blender and process until completely mixed. Turn off, add the rest of your ingredients except for the vanilla bean, if using, and blend until totally emulsified. If using the vanilla bean, split the bean in half and scrape out the vanilla pods.

[EARTHY/GREEN]

These recipes are hearty on the low down. They're light, refreshing, but very satiating. Lots of these can double as soups in a jar to make your life easier.

DEEP Pulse

2 SERVINGS — LEVEL II, LG, SB, NF

Savory smoothies are great on-the-go lunch and dinner options. You can eat them with a spoon like soup. Leafy greens and garlic are superfoods, filled with antioxidants and anti-inflammatory properties so that you can't go wrong with them. Hemp seeds provide a protein boost and the avocado has all the right kinds of fatty acids.

INGREDIENTS:

1 large handful of spinach, or any other leafy green
1 yellow or orange bell pepper
½ avocado
2 garlic cloves, peeled
2 tomatoes
½ to 1 cup water
⅛ onion
Pinch of sea salt
1 tbsp sesame seeds
1 tbsp hemp seeds
¼ cup extra virgin olive oil
Handful of ice cubes (optional, for a thicker smoothie)

DIRECTIONS:

Wash all produce well and cut into chunks. Pulverize sesame seeds and hemp seeds in a coffee grinder or with a mortar and pestle for best results. Blend all ingredients until silky smooth. Enjoy right away and feel hella good about it.

The Herbaceous Kind

I'm into this smoothie as a dinner or lunch option since it's practically a salad/gazpacho situation. The veg provides plenty of vitamins A, K, and C, not to mention fiber (since this is blended and not juiced).

INGREDIENTS:

1 handful of salad greens (Boston, Bibb, or romaine lettuce are best in this recipe)

3 vine-ripened Roma tomatoes

4 sprigs fresh cilantro

4 sprigs fresh parsley

2 tbsp fresh basil

2 tbsp fresh dill

1 celery stalk

½ cup water (optional, depending on how juicy your tomatoes are)

Squeeze of lime juice

Small handful of ice cubes (optional, for a thicker smoothie)

Pinch of salt

DIRECTIONS:

Throw all ingredients into your blender and puree until smooth and delicious.

Life's Chard

1-2 SERVINGS
LEVEL II, LG, NF, SB, AI

Don't be so chard on yourself, you look great! And you'll feel even better once your bod is flooded with all the amazing benefits of Swiss chard. This leafy green is an excellent source of vitamins K, A, and C, as well as magnesium, copper, manganese, potassium, and calcium. Let's not forget our healthy bowel movement BFF, fiber.

INGREDIENTS:

1 cup coconut water
½ cucumber
1 pear
½ lime, peeled
1 bunch of chard
1" chunk of fresh ginger
Handful of ice (optional)

DIRECTIONS:

Wash all produce well and cut into smaller chunks that'll fit into your blender. Blend until everything's smooth and delicious.

Feeling Blossom

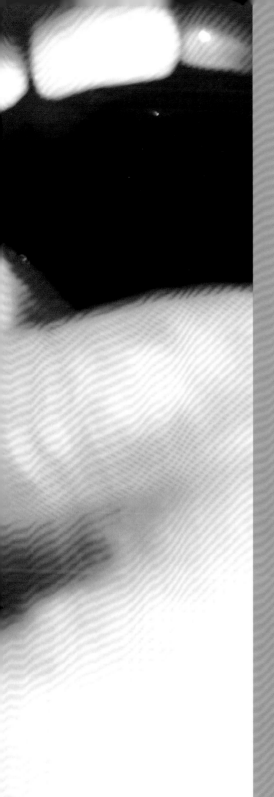

1-2 SERVINGS — LEVEL I, AI

Cherries have manifold benefits, but my fave is that they support healthy sleep since they contain melatonin. Don't worry, it won't make you sleepy, but it'll make sure you catch some healthy ZzZzZzZs at night! You don't necessarily have to freeze the cherries, but it just gives the smoothie some extra richness and thickness. If using fresh cherries, add a handful of ice cubes to add thickness.

INGREDIENTS:

2 handfuls of fresh spinach
1 cup frozen cherries, pitted
½ cup water
2 tbsp almond butter
½ tsp ginger
½ tsp cinnamon

DIRECTIONS:

Blend all ingredients together until silky smooth.

Salad-in-a-jar

2 SERVINGS — LEVEL II, LG, SB, NF, AI

Forget the Pinterest salad in a jar! This is literally a salad in a jar that just happens to be blended up too. It's delicious and reminiscent of a Bloody Mary or soup, or a little of both. Enjoy on days when you gotta eat like the healthy human you are but you just don't have the fucking time.

INGREDIENTS:

1½ cups tomatoes, firmly packed
½ cup fresh parsley
⅔ cup water
½ avocado
1 tbsp lime juice
2 tsp extra virgin olive oil
3 sun-dried tomatoes
¾ tsp sea salt
Pinch of cayenne
Pinch of black pepper
Handful of ice cubes (optional)
2 tsp red onion, finely chopped, for garnish

DIRECTIONS:

Blend all ingredients except the red onion together until smooth. Garnish with the red onions. Enjoy right away.

Touch Me, Please

DID YA KNOW?

Figs have wasps inside of them . . . what? Yup. Fig trees only bear the fruit thanks to fig wasps, tiny wasps that are born inside figs. When female fig wasps hatch, they crawl out to find another fig where they can lay their own eggs. But, don't worry: as the fig ripens, it basically digests the dead wasps inside so what you're tasting is just fig! Phew.

4 SERVINGS
LEVEL 1, LG, SB, AI, NF

This smoothie combines everything you need into one glass—greens, fruit, and ginger—to give your digestion a break and to get your bod to work cleansing.

INGREDIENTS:

Small bunch of collard green leaves
Small bunch of kale leaves
Small bunch of parsley
1½ Asian pears
½ pear
1" chunk of fresh ginger, depending on how spicy you desire it
6 to 8 figs
½ cup water
¼ cup ice cubes

DIRECTIONS:

Blend all ingredients until smooth.

Will You Matcha Me?

2 SERVINGS — LEVEL I, LG, NF, AI

Matcha is a type of green tea that's traditional in Japanese culture. It's a beautiful green color and has an insane amount of benefits: it's one of the highest sources of antioxidants, calms you down so you can chill out, boosts memory, and helps you focus thanks to an amino acid called L-theanine, and it energizes you.

INGREDIENTS:

2 Asian pears, chopped
1 tbsp pure matcha tea powder
1 cup water
3 to 5 pitted dates
½ tsp vanilla extract
Pinch of salt
Handful of ice cubes

DIRECTIONS:

Blend all ingredients together

[SPICY SMOOTHIES]

These fiery options are sure to spice up your diet. These are awesome energy boosts that are sure to give ya a kick in ya booty (in the best way possible).

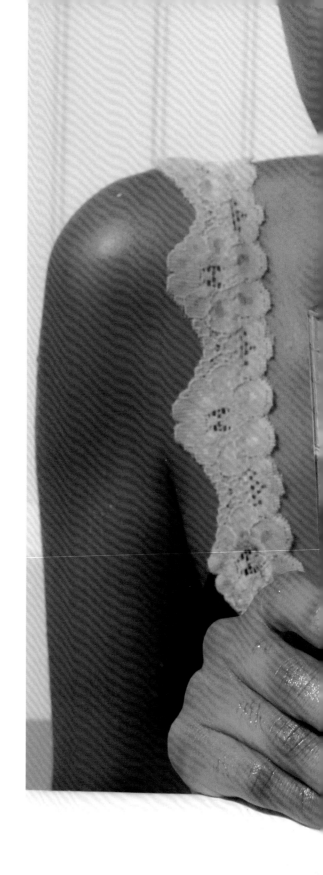

Chai Life

Chai is a delicious blend of spices that's so comforting, especially combined with creamy cashew mylk. Don't be afraid to adjust according to your preferences! Adding 1 tablespoon of nut butter would make this creamier and even heartier.

INGREDIENTS:

2 frozen bananas
¼ cup cashew mylk (page 216)
¼ tsp vanilla extract
¼ tsp cinnamon
Pinch ground cloves
1 tsp fresh ginger, grated
1 cup water
Pinch of pepper

DIRECTIONS:

Add all ingredients to your blender except the pepper and puree until smooth. Add a pinch of pepper before drinking. Enjoy.

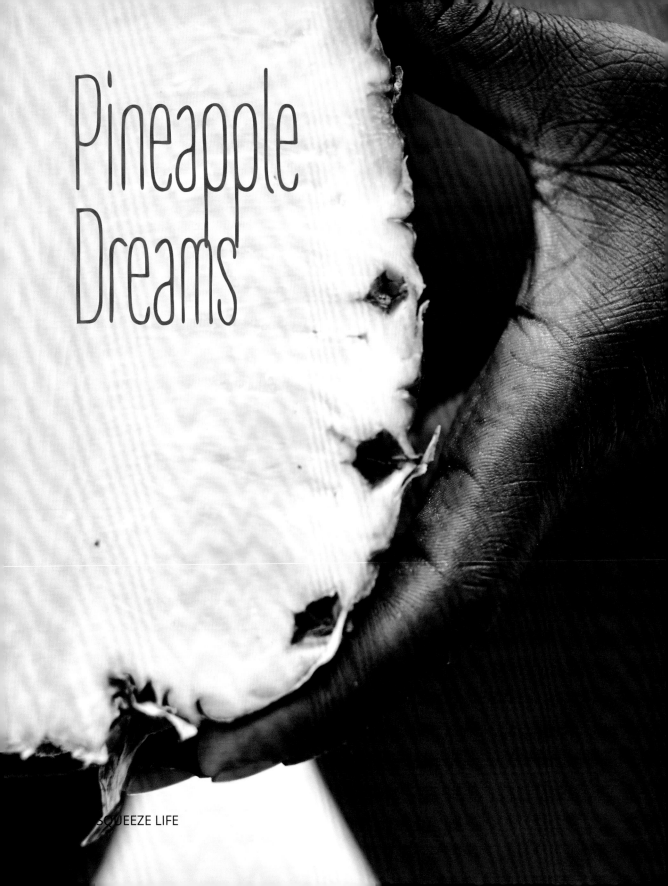

Pineapple Dreams

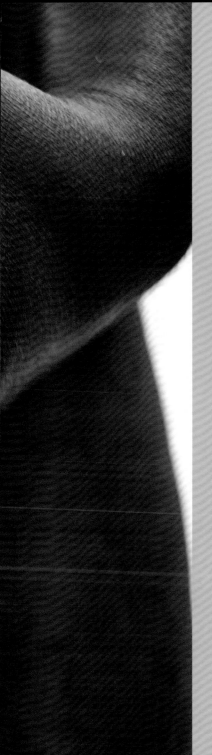

This dreamboat of a smoothie does wonders in reducing inflammation and soothing your bod in general. Bromelain, a digestive enzyme found in pineapple, helps to treat inflammation and it can also help with digestive problems. Any spicy smoothie is great for clearing up congestion.

INGREDIENTS:

1 cup coconut water
2½ cups diced pineapple, frozen works best
Small bunch of collard greens, or
any other kind of leafy green
¼ cucumber
1½ tsp finely chopped red onion
3 sprigs of parsley
1 tsp finely chopped jalapeño
2 tbsp fresh lime juice
Pinch of lime zest
¼ cup ice cubes (omit if using frozen pineapples)
Pinch of sea salt

DIRECTIONS:

Blend all ingredients using a high-speed blender on high until smooth and creamy. Feel free to tweak the flavors according to your taste (more jalapeño, lime juice, etc.).

PICO de MANGO green SMOOTHIE

2 SERVINGS — LEVEL I, AI, SB, NF

Mangoes are great for the skin! They clear pores and eliminate acne. Gulp, gulp, gulp!

INGREDIENTS:

1½ cups coconut water OR water

2 frozen mangoes

Large handful of chard, or any other leafy green

2 tsp chopped red onion

¼ cucumber

Small bunch of cilantro

1 tsp chopped jalapeño

1 large lime, juiced

¼ tsp sea salt

1 cup ice cubes, if not using frozen mangoes

DIRECTIONS:

Blend all ingredients together until smooth and creamy.

Curry in a Flurry

This unique smoothie is reminiscent of a curry, but still manages to be very refreshing with hints of citrus. Turmeric has incredible anti-inflammatory powers so I recommend drinking this to reduce any joint pain especially for those with rheumatoid arthritis and osteoarthritis!

INGREDIENTS:

2 cups coconut mylk (see page 215 or 218)
2 cups mango, frozen works best
½ cup coconut meat
1 peach
1 tbsp lime juice
½ tsp lime zest
½ tsp yellow curry powder
1 tbsp freshly juiced turmeric OR
1 tsp dried turmeric powder
Pinch of red pepper flakes
Pinch of sea salt
½ to 1 cup ice cubes, less if
using frozen mangoes

DIRECTIONS:

Blend all ingredients in a blender until smooth and creamy. Feel free to adjust any ingredients to best suit your preferences.

[FRUITY SMOOTHIES]

These recipes are basically healthy
slushies. Need I say more?

HOW MANY
JUICES
TIL SOHO?

2-3 SERVINGS — LEVEL I, SB, NF

Babes, I want you to be stimulated in ways you haven't before. Let's get weird and use some spearmint to get your blood pumping. "Wait, did you just say spearmint? How anticlimactic." Au contraire, s-mint is insanely refreshing and energizing! This blend gives you amazing clarity and fills you with vitamins A, B_1, B_2, B_6, C, E, and K, as well as protein, calcium, iron, phytonutrients, and beta-carotene.

INGREDIENTS:

4 cups blueberries, frozen
1 banana, frozen
1 cup fresh spearmint tea, chilled
Handful of mint
½ tsp cinnamon
Handful of ice cubes

DIRECTIONS:

Blend all ingredients together in a high-speed blender until silky smooth. Enjoy your blue balls!

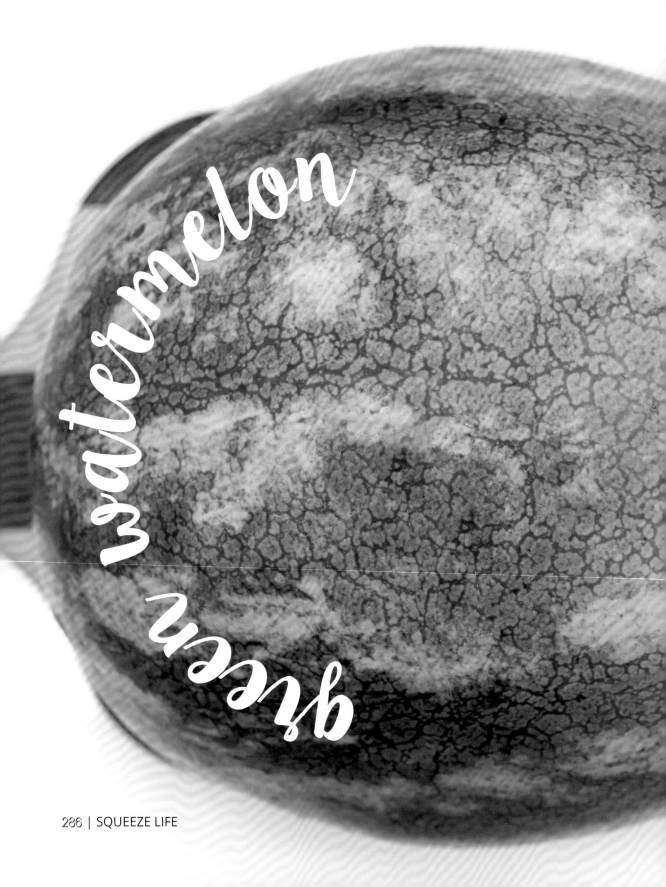

green watermelon

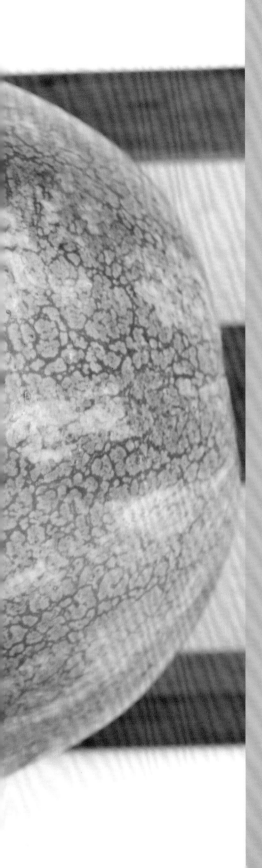

2-4 SERVINGS — LEVEL II, NF, AI, SB

Watermelon is nearly all water, duh, and for that reason it's extremely refreshing and hydrating. It contains lots of vitamins A, B_6, C, and antioxidants. Lycopene is a wonderful antioxidant found in watermelon that has been proven to reduce cardiovascular issues.

INGREDIENTS:

1 cup arugula

6 cups watermelon chunks, frozen works best

1 pear

½ cup coconut water

Pinch of sea salt

DIRECTIONS:

Blend all ingredients together until smooth and creamy.

FIRST BLUSH

2 SERVINGS — LEVEL II, SB, NF

This is the ultimate summer treat: refreshing, hydrating, and so pretty in a pitcher (especially if said pitcher is at the beach or chilling on a front porch). Hibiscus is known to have some amazing cardiovascular benefits! It can relax you and lower your blood pressure, which can lower your risk for heart disease and stroke. Not to mention hibiscus tea is packed with antioxidants that are your bod's best friend for so many reasons.

INGREDIENTS:

2 cups hibiscus tea, chilled

½ cup strawberries, frozen

½ cup frozen raspberries, frozen

1 banana, frozen

2 dates, pitted

10 fresh mint leaves (optional)

DIRECTIONS:

Blend all ingredients until smooth.

Honey Pot

The combo of honeydew and coconut water makes this smoothie super hydrating and FRESH! Like, whoa. Honeydew is known to contain both vitamin C and copper, which promote healthy skin by helping in collagen production.

INGREDIENTS:

¼ head romaine lettuce
½ cup honeydew chunks
½ frozen banana
5 mint leaves
½ cup coconut water
Lime zest
1 cup ice

DIRECTIONS:

Blend everything until smooth and creamy.

mango

COCONUT

2 SERVINGS — LEVEL II, NF, SB, AI

This smoothie is a mini vacation—let it take you away! Mango adds a slight sweetness to this refreshing flavor bomb.

INGREDIENTS:

½ cup frozen mango
½ cup coconut meat
1 lime, juiced
Handful of cilantro
1 cup coconut water
Handful of ice cubes

DIRECTIONS:

Blend all ingredients until super smooth.

Strawberry Daydream

2 SERVINGS — LEVEL 1, NF, AI, SB

If this smoothie was a song, it'd be sung by Katy Perry. For sure. It's sweet and refreshing with some complex flavors from the basil leaves. It looks pretty in a pitcher or carafe so don't miss out on the opportunity to impress someone next time you're hosting a brunch.

INGREDIENTS:

2 cups strawberries
2 nectarines, pitted
1 mango, pitted
1 banana
½ cup fresh basil
1 cup water

DIRECTIONS:

Blend all ingredients until smooth.
Feel free to add a handful of ice
and pulse at the very end for a
colder, thicker smoothie.

Orange Creamsicle Smoothie

1-2 SERVINGS — LEVEL I, SB, NF

Insert nostalgic remarks about how this tastes like your childhood. Seriously, this amazing smoothie will totally take you back to the days when you were a tiny peanut, stumbling about with melted ice cream all over your face.

INGREDIENTS:

1 frozen ripe banana

½ cup coconut meat

2 oranges, peeled and with the seeds removed

1 tbsp coconut butter OR coconut oil

3 dates, pitted

1 cup coconut mylk OR almond mylk OR coconut water

DIRECTIONS:

Combine all ingredients in a blender until silky smooth. Serve right away.

Ginger-Mango chai SMOOTHIE

1-2 SERVINGS — LEVEL 1, SB, NF, AI

Chai is traditionally taken after meals as a digestive and it has fantastic digestive boosting effects. Black pepper, ginger, and cinnamon are all known to stimulate healthy digestion and this smoothie's got them all for an ultra soothing feeling!

INGREDIENTS:

1 cup frozen mango
1 tsp freshly grated ginger
½ frozen banana
⅔ cup coconut mylk
1 tsp cinnamon
¼ tsp cardamom
¼ tsp nutmeg
¼ tsp ground cloves
Pinch of black pepper
Handful of ice cubes

DIRECTIONS:

Blend all ingredients until smooth. Feel free to add any optional ingredients for a more flavorful chai.

Sweet Sinner

2-3 SERVINGS — LEVEL II, AI, NF, SB

This smoothie is packed with protein from the help of flaxseed/hemp seeds and leafy greens. Oranges, mango, and pineapple add a nice sweetness, but also plenty of vitamin C.

INGREDIENTS:

1 mango

1 tbsp coconut oil

2 tbsp flaxseed meal or ground hemp seeds

1 cup water

2 oranges, peeled

1 cup pineapple

Large handful of kale, or any other leafy green (optional)

2 tbsp fresh ginger root, chopped

1 cup ice (optional)

DIRECTIONS:

Add all ingredients into your blender and puree until smooth and creamy.

Pop
Your
Cherry

1 SERVING — LEVEL II, NF, SB

Let this smoothie satiate you and meet your quota for protein, omega fatty acids, and vitamin A!

INGREDIENTS:

1 cup fresh or frozen cherries, pitted
1½ oranges, peeled
Handful of kale, chopped
2 tbsp hemp seeds
1 tbsp raw coconut oil
1 cup ice

DIRECTIONS:

Blend all ingredients in your blender and enjoy right away.

Watermelon Mojito

2 SERVINGS — LEVEL II, NF, SB

What can be better? This drink is easy, almost a little too easy. But don't get suspicious . . . it's easy because it includes the best ingredients that momma nature has to offer.

INGREDIENTS:

4 cups watermelon, frozen will give you a creamier texture
8 fresh mint leaves
1 lime, juiced

DIRECTIONS:

Blend all ingredients together until smooth and delicious. If using fresh watermelon, pulse in a handful of ice at the very end to ensure ultimate refresh-ability.

Apple, Spice & Everything Nice

This may seem like a weird combo at first . . . I mean, apples and rosemary? What. Just think of it as the best fall-inspired drink ever. It's warming and cozy without being heavy.

INGREDIENTS:

2 large apples, cored
½ mango
1 cup mylk, whatever your fave is
2 tsp fresh rosemary, chopped
½ tsp vanilla extract
Pinch of cayenne

DIRECTIONS:

Blend all ingredients until smooth.

FEELIN' MYSELF

2 SERVINGS — LEVEL I, AI, SB, NF

Get ready to really feel yourself, 'cause this smoothie will make ya feel good and look good! It's sweet with a little green and a teeny bit of cayenne to get things flowing for ya. Feel free to use collards, chards, or spinach in this recipe.

INGREDIENTS:

2 cups frozen strawberries
1 tbsp coconut oil
2 tbsp flaxseed meal OR ground hemp seeds
Large handful of fresh mint leaves
1 cup water
⅛ tsp cayenne pepper
1 cup pineapple chunks
2 oranges, peeled
1 cup chopped greens
1 cup ice cubes (optional)

DIRECTIONS:

Add all ingredients into your blender and puree until smooth and creamy.

So Vanilla

1 SERVING — LEVEL I, AI, NF

This smoothie is so vanilla, but so not boring! Tahini adds a nice creaminess, some extra protein, and a boatload of minerals (phosphorus, magnesium, potassium, and iron), meaning you'll be satiated and detoxified.

INGREDIENTS:

1 cup mylk, whatever your fave is

1 frozen banana

3 tbsp tahini OR sesame seeds

1 date, pitted

1 tsp white chia seeds, best if ground

Pinch of cinnamon

½ tsp vanilla extract

Handful of ice cubes

DIRECTIONS:

Blend all ingredients until smooth and creamy.

LUNCH & DINNER

[SOUPS]

RAWnchy soups are life-changing. Hearty, comforting, but still RAWesome.

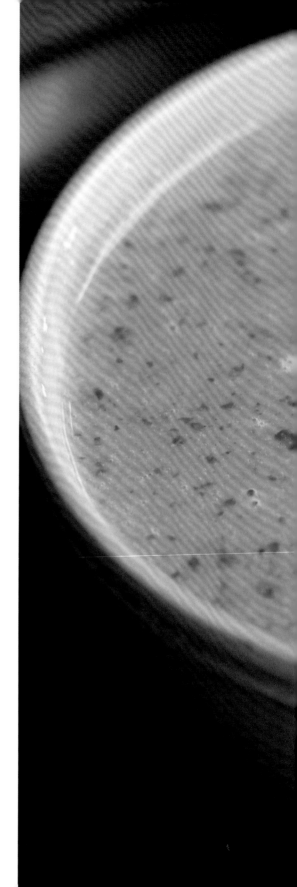

GREEN **power** ZUCCHINI *with* FUSILLI

INGREDIENTS:

1 large zucchini, chopped

1 bunch of leafy greens, whatever you like best (chard, kale, etc.)

1 tbsp lemon juice

2 tbsp Bragg Liquid Aminos

¼ tsp sea salt

½ avocado, chopped

⅔ tbsp fresh rosemary (optional)

½ to 1 cup water

1 tbsp mellow white miso

1 garlic clove, peeled

1 tbsp olive oil

4 SERVINGS
LEVEL 1, LG, SB, NF

Zucchini is truly magical when blended and pureed. It's the silkiest veg around. This soup is the anti-soup, really. It's refreshing and incredibly light. The zuke fusilli adds an extra heartiness and texture to the dish. Bragg Liquid Aminos adds a deep savory flavor, but better yet, it adds a boost of healthy plant-based protein in the form of 16 different amino acids.

DIRECTIONS:

Puree all ingredients until silky smooth.

For the zucchini fusilli:
1 zucchini
1 garlic clove, peeled and minced
Olive oil
Salt, to taste

DIRECTIONS:

Wash the zucchini well. Using a spiralizer or mandoline set on the thinnest setting, slice the zucchini into noodle-like strands. If you don't have a spiralizer or mandoline, you can slice the zuke with a knife as thinly as possible. Toss with enough olive oil and minced garlic to lightly coat the zuke and season with salt. Marinate for 30 minutes to an hour until softened. Serve the zuke fusilli on top of your soup.

Avocado Gazpacho

4 SERVINGS — LEVEL 1, SB, NF, AI, LG

Who doesn't love avocado? This soup's my love letter to avocado, and to you. All those fatty oils from the beloved avo are amazing for your skin and hair.

DID YA KNOW?
If you fantasize of having a baby, anything with basil (which has plenty of folate) is good for fetal cell growth and division. It's just basic math.

INGREDIENTS:

For the gazpacho:
3 large tomatoes
1 large cucumber
⅓ cup fresh basil, packed
1 lime, juiced
1 tbsp miso
3 tbsp olive oil

For the avocado salsa:
1 avocado, diced
1 tsp minced jalapeño
Salt and pepper
1 tbsp minced onion
2 tbsp cilantro leaves, chopped

DIRECTIONS:

Using a food processor or blender, puree all gazpacho ingredients until silky smooth. Combine all avocado salsa ingredients together. Chill before serving. Serve chilled gazpacho with some of the salsa and a drizzle of olive oil, if you'd like.

APPLE

celery

BITCHY-SSOISE

4 SERVINGS — LEVEL I, SB, AI

Vichyssoise is traditionally a cold soup made of pureed leeks, onions, potatoes, cream, and chicken stock, but this is a raw, detox-friendly version for the babeliest babes who are craving a satiating soup. It's cashew-creamy but still insanely refreshing and perfect on a hot, steamy night—not to mention easy.

INGREDIENTS:

2 celery stalks
1 cup apple juice
1 cup celery juice
1 tbsp onion, chopped
2 cloves garlic
½ cup raw cashews
1 cup water
¼ cup olive oil
1 tbsp lemon juice
¼ tsp pepper
¼ tsp coriander
Sea salt, to taste

DIRECTIONS:

Using a mandoline, slice the celery into thin ribbons. Set aside. Blend all ingredients, except celery ribbons, until smooth. Stir in celery ribbons and serve.

I Love Spicy Gingers

I love spicy gingers! And this soup's not bad either . . . get it? This sweet and spicy gazpacho is the best way to take your dose of beta-carotene. Ginger and the cayenne pepper get your blood pumping in the best way possible to kick-start healthy circulation.

INGREDIENTS:

1 cup carrot juice
1 avocado
2 tbsp hemp seeds
1 tbsp chopped ginger
1 tsp sea salt
¼ tsp cayenne pepper
2 tbsp maple syrup OR coconut nectar
1 tbsp tahini
2 tbsp extra virgin olive oil, for garnish
Avocado slices, for garnish

DIRECTIONS:

Using a food processor or blender, puree all ingredients, except olive oil and avocado slices, until silky smooth. Serve with extra avocado slices and a drizzle of olive oil.

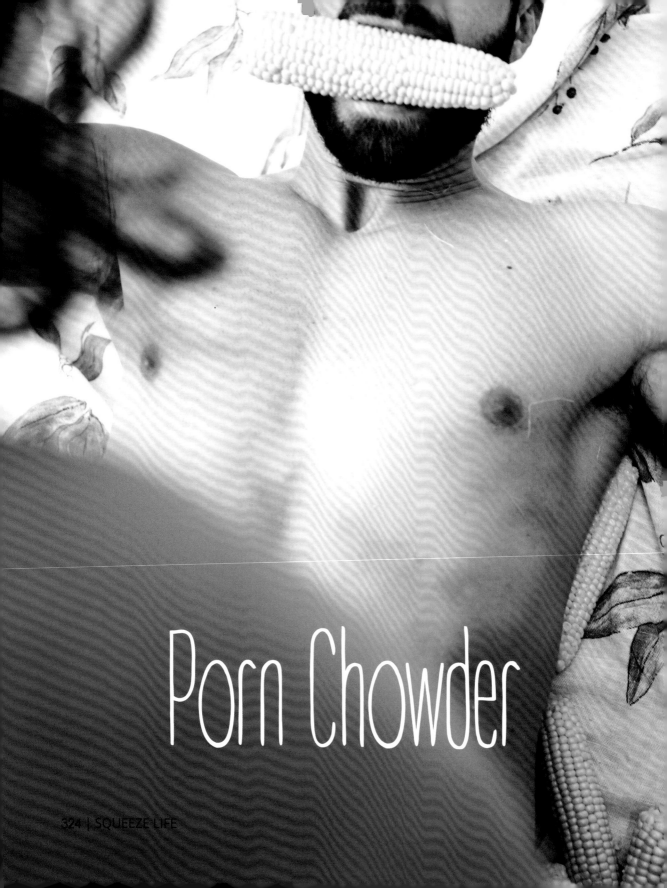

Porn Chowder

4 SERVINGS — LEVEL I, AI

Traditional corn chowder is clogged with cream, much like your bod after consuming it. So do yourself a huge favor and try this clean version instead. It's best made in the summer when corn is sweet and thriving. Cashews give it a creaminess that'll make ya cream while you forget about cream (if ya get what I mean).

INGREDIENTS:

3½ cups fresh yellow corn kernels, about 4 ears of corn

2 cups water

⅔ cup raw cashews OR pine nuts

6 tbsp extra virgin olive oil

1 garlic clove

2 tsp sea salt

2 tbsp maple syrup OR coconut nectar

2 tsp ancho chili powder

1 tbsp chopped chives, tarragon, parsley, or cilantro

Fresh ground pepper, to taste

DIRECTIONS:

In a blender or food processor, combine 2¼ cups of the corn with the water, cashews, olive oil, maple syrup or coconut nectar, garlic, and salt, and then puree until smooth. Ladle the soup into bowls and garnish with the remaining corn kernels, herbs, and black pepper. Serve right away. This corn chowder can be made ahead of time and refrigerated overnight for up to 3 days.

Roasted Red Pepper Immunity

2-4 SERVINGS — LEVEL 1, LG, SB, AI

This garlicky bisque does the body good. Wondrous raw garlic boosts your immune system and contains manganese, vitamin B$_6$, vitamin C, selenium, calcium, iron, and more! Not to mention it's hella tasty, especially with some 'cado cubes on top.

INGREDIENTS:

1½ cups water
½ chipotle pepper, rehydrated in water
2 red bell peppers
1½ tomatoes
2 sun-dried tomatoes, rehydrated in water
½ avocado
2 garlic cloves
5 tbsp extra virgin olive oil
1 to 2 tsp sea salt, to taste
½ cup cashews
A handful of basil leaves (optional)
A handful of cilantro leaves (optional)
Black pepper (optional)

DIRECTIONS:

Using a food processor or blender, puree until creamy and smooth. Top with any optional garnishes, if desired. I love to crumble FUNyons (see page 374) on top of the creamy soup for crunch and texture.

Creamy Butternut Squash Soup with Ginger Basil Crème Fraîche

4 SERVINGS — LEVEL 1, AI, SB

Who thought that you could still soup it out while keeping it raw? Well, my babies, you can! This recipe has all the creamy, silky goodness of your fave b-squash soup minus all the ingredients that stick to your ribs . . . in the worst way possible.

INGREDIENTS:

½ cup apple cider vinegar

½ cup water (for marinade)

1 medium butternut squash, peeled

4 cups water (for blending)

¼ cup raw cashews

¼ cup olive oil

1 tbsp lemon juice

2 tbsp miso

1 tsp cumin

1 tsp pepper

1 tsp salt

DIRECTIONS:

Combine the apple cider vinegar and water. Cut the butternut squash into 2-inch cubes and marinate in diluted apple cider vinegar for 2 hours. Rinse and set in freezer until frozen. Thaw butternut squash.

Blend all remaining ingredients until smooth. Feel free to add extra water a little bit at a time to reach a silky puree consistency. Serve with a dollop of Ginger Basil Crème Fraîche (see page 330).

Ginger Basil Creme Fraîche

This dreamy cream is lusciously fresh and perfect for dolloping on your favorite raw soups. It may or may not also be delicious eaten off of attractive bodies, à la sexy sushi.

INGREDIENTS:

1 cup cashews, soaked
½ cup water
¼ cup coconut oil
1 tbsp lemon juice
2 tbsp ginger juice
¼ cup fresh basil leaves
½ tsp sea salt

DIRECTIONS:

Using a food processor or blender, blend until creamy and smooth.

[SOLID FARE]

Who knew you could eat so well while cleansing? Well, I did. Which is why I wrote this book. *Duh*, you guys . . .

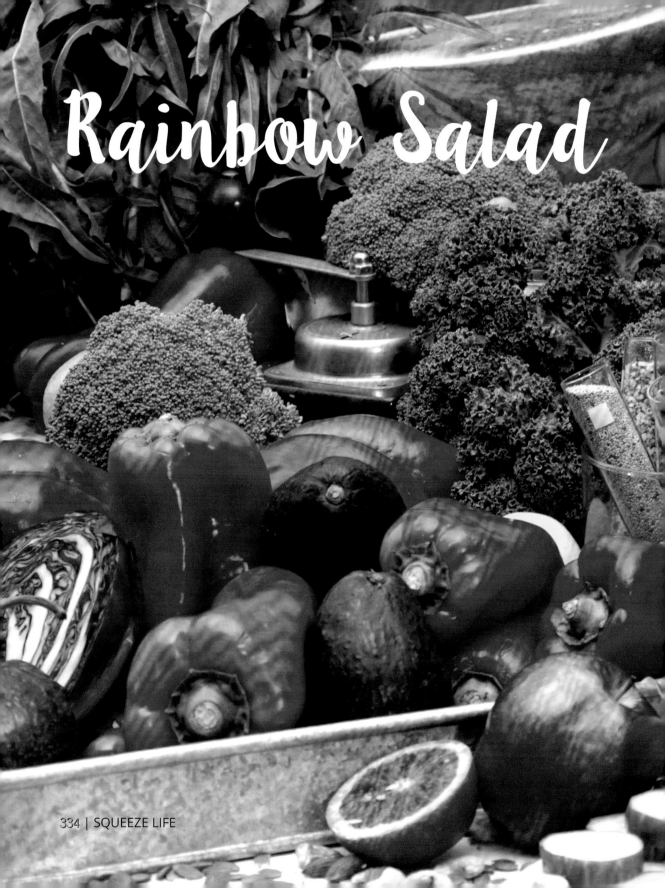

Rainbow Salad

1-2 SERVINGS
LEVEL 1, SB, LG, AI, NF

Tasting the rainbow just got a lot RAW-nchier thanks to this babe-inducing salad. Not only is it visually beautiful, but your taste buds will thank you. There's tons of protein, and vitamins, not to mention different textures, to keep you interested until the very last bite. Use this as a guide and swap whatever's fresh to create a new salad.

INGREDIENTS:

1 head of lettuce, chopped

2 tbsp pumpkin seeds

2 tbsp hemp seeds

1 carrot, shredded

½ red bell pepper, sliced into matchsticks

1 small wedge of cabbage (purple for color) shredded

4 kale leaves, roughly chopped

2 shallots, finely chopped

1 avocado, cubed

1 small cucumber, chopped

4 tbsp extra virgin olive oil

½ lemon, juiced

DIRECTIONS:

Toss all ingredients together until the olive oil and lemon juice are well incorporated with the produce. Serve right away.

CITRUS KALE *salad* WITH *avocado* DRESSING

1-2 SERVINGS — LEVEL I, AI, NF, LG

We all love kale, but my fave part about this salad is the rich and creamy dressing that perfectly coats all those kale leaves. It also holds up well if made ahead of time.

INGREDIENTS:

For the dressing:

1 avocado

1 lemon, juiced

1 lime, juiced

3 tbsp hazelnut oil OR extra virgin olive oil

¼ to ½ tsp sea salt

1 garlic clove

1 tbsp red onion

1 bunch of kale, stripped off the stem and chopped

1 large handful of parsley, chopped

DIRECTIONS:

In a food processor or blender, process all the ingredients for the dressing until emulsified. Marinate the kale in the dressing. Make sure to rub the dressing into the kale so it's massaged and softened a bit. Toss all the ingredients together and enjoy.

If making ahead of time, simply toss everything together. No need to marinate the kale in the dressing, since you'll be saving it for later.

Summer Dreamin' Rolls

2-4 SERVINGS — LEVEL I, SB

These rolls will get your bod ready for summer! They're ideal for a light lunch, dinner, or even as party snaxxx. Don't be intimidated by the lengthy recipe, it's actually super easy to make (and even easier to eat)! For some extra hearty protein, serve with the Peanutty Almond Sauce (see page 340).

INGREDIENTS:

1 package of rice paper wraps (both round or square wraps work, but this won't be RAWnchy) OR make your own Coconut Wrappers (see page 342)

1 mango, peeled and thinly sliced into matchsticks

1 avocado, peeled and thinly sliced into matchsticks

1 bell pepper, thinly sliced into matchsticks

1 cucumber, sliced into matchsticks

Handful of mint, finely chopped

Bunch of scallions, finely chopped

Water

DIRECTIONS:

There isn't a *right* way of making these rolls, it's just really assembling and rolling. Just make sure all your ingredients are ready to go, and you have an assembly line in front of you. That way you can just assemble and roll.

Fill a bowl with water. If you are using the rice paper wraps, you will need to soak them with water so they become pliable. Soak as you go, for a minute or so. If you are using the Coconut Wrappers you don't need to soak them. Just make sure they are at room temperature.

Grab a wrapper and assemble a bit of filling on the edge that's closest to you. Gently pull the edge closest to you over the filling and begin rolling it tightly (like a tiny burrito). You can choose to keep the ends open, or tuck them in (using water if you need more "glue").

Repeat until either all the filling or wrappers are done. Serve with Peanutty Almond Sauce (page 340).

PEANUTTY *almond* SAUCE

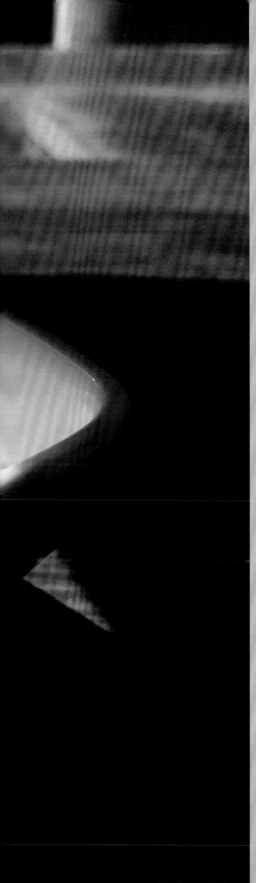

This sauce is perfection with the Summer Dreamin' Rolls, but it's so good that you'll want it everywhere! Serve with zucchini noodles and veggies for a quick dinner.

INGREDIENTS:

¼ cup Liquid Bragg Aminos OR tamari

1 tbsp lime juice

1 tbsp minced ginger

1 garlic clove, minced

2 tbsp coconut sugar OR maple syrup

⅛ tsp chili flakes

2 tbsp rice vinegar OR apple cider vinegar

1 tbsp sesame oil OR extra virgin olive oil

¼ cup almond butter OR Wild Jungle Peanut Butter for a completely raw version

DIRECTIONS:

Using a food processor or blender, puree all ingredients until silky smooth.

Coconut Wrappers

YIELDS 3-4 SHEETS — LEVEL 1, SB, NF

Coconut wrappers are here for all yer wrapping needs! These are so versatile and can be used just like you would a tortilla or wrap—make some RAWsome burritos, veg wraps, and spring rolls FOR DAYS.

INGREDIENTS:

4 cups young coconut meat, chopped
½ tsp sea salt
¼ cup coconut water

DIRECTIONS:

Using a blender or food processor, mix all ingredients until it forms a paste. Spread the mixture over a dehydrator sheet and dehydrate for 4–5 hours. If you don't have a dehydrator, spread the mixture on a baking sheet coated with a thin layer of coconut oil. Bake at 225°F for 1.5-2 hours or until wrap is thoroughly dry. Remove from dehydrator and trim the outer edges of each sheet to make it even, then cut each sheet into squares or circles (depending on the size of your summer rolls). Wrap in plastic and store in the refrigerator for up to 3 days.

Prior to using, remove from the fridge and allow to come to room temperature.

Faux-lafel

8–14 FAUX-LAFELS, DEPENDING ON SIZE – LEVEL I, SB, LG

Falafel is a dreamy food, except when it's fried. This version is an ode to the classic, and an ode to your wondrous body. Here's to not polluting your insides with fried, fatty foods! Cheers!

INGREDIENTS:

1½ cups almonds
½ cup pumpkin seeds
½ cup fresh cilantro
¼ cup fresh parsley
4 tbsp lemon juice
2 tbsp tahini
1 tbsp olive oil
1½ tsp ground cumin
1 tsp sea salt
¾ cup water

DIRECTIONS:

Pulse almonds in a food processor until fine. Add the remaining ingredients and process until thoroughly mixed. Roll the mixture into small balls and place on a mesh dehydrator screen, dehydrating for 4 hours. If using a conventional oven, set temp to 225°F for approximately 45 minutes-1 hour. Serve with the tahini on a bed of your fave falafel fixins or whatever kind of lettuce and tomatoes you have in your bitchin' kitchen.

TAHINI SAUCE

INGREDIENTS:

For the tahini:
½ cup tahini
¼ cup olive oil
¼ cup water
2 tbsp lemon juice
1 chipotle chile, seeds removed (optional)
2 dates
1 tsp ground cumin
1 tsp ground coriander
1 tsp sea salt

DIRECTIONS:

Blend all ingredients until smooth.

Avocado-Stuffed Dates Wrapped with Eggplant Fakin'

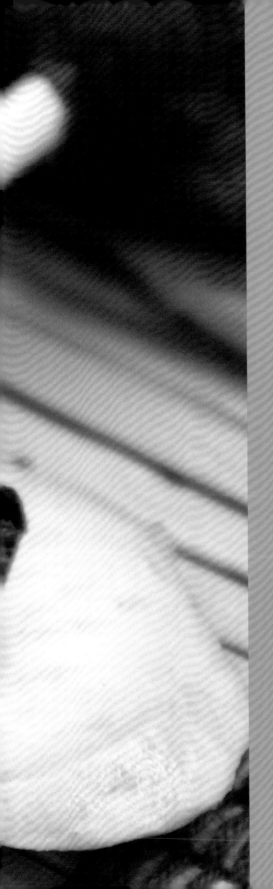

20 PIECES — LEVEL 1, NF

Yeah, you read that right. Just 'cause you care about your insides it doesn't mean you can't wrap food in fakin' bacon. These are a powerhouse of energy! Dates are a great source of fiber and a good food to eat to guarantee good times on the pooper (they promote great bowel movements). Avos are America's sweetheart and they provide healthy fats that will make ya hair and skin look great.

INGREDIENTS:

1 avocado, pitted and cut into about 20 small chunks

20 medjool dates, pitted

1 batch Eggplant Fakin' (see page 348), cut into 1"- thick strips

DIRECTIONS:

Place a chunk of avocado inside each date. Wrap a strip of fakin' around each date and roll, using a toothpick to keep everything in place. Serve right away and enjoy!

Eggplant Fakin'

INGREDIENTS:

1 tbsp Bragg Liquid Aminos OR tamari

2 tbsp maple syrup

2 tbsp apple cider vinegar

2 tbsp extra virgin olive oil

1 tsp chili powder

½ tsp smoked paprika

½ tsp garlic powder

½ tsp sea salt

Black pepper, to taste

1 large eggplant, peeled and sliced into ¼" slices

DIRECTIONS:

Combine all ingredients, except for the eggplant slices, until well mixed. Marinate the eggplant slices in the mix for about 1 hour.

Place the marinated slices into a dehydrator at 115°F until completely dry, about 12 hours. You can dehydrate it longer if you like crispier fakin'.

If you don't have a dehydrator, bake the marinade eggplant at 350°F for 18 minutes, making sure to occasionally baste them with additional marinade to keep things juicy.

Beet Carpaccio with Pumpkin Seed Pâté

Oh, look who's fancy now! Unlike beef crapaccio, this beet version is immune-boosting and promotes healthy muscle function thanks to vitamin C, potassium, fiber, and other essential minerals found in this purple root. The Lemon Garlic Vinaigrette is also amazing for salads!

INGREDIENTS:

3 peeled beets

1 recipe Lemon Garlic Vinaigrette (see page 352)

1 recipe Pumpkin Seed Pâté (see page 353)

DIRECTIONS:

Using a mandoline, slice the beets into ¼-inch slices. Marinate in the Lemon Garlic Vinaigrette for at least 1 hour and then freeze for a few hours. Thaw when ready to serve. Top with Pumpkin Seed Pâté and devour.

INGREDIENTS:

1 cup extra virgin olive oil

⅓ cup lemon juice

3 garlic cloves

½ tsp black pepper

1 tsp sea salt

DIRECTIONS:

In a blender or food processor, emulsify all ingredients. If not using right away, keep in the fridge in an airtight jar for up to a week.

Lemon Garlic Vinaigrette

Pumpkin Seed Pâté

INGREDIENTS:

3 cups pumpkin seeds, soaked for 3 hours

¼ cup miso

½ cup water

¼ cup extra virgin olive oil

1 tbsp lemon juice

½ tsp sea salt

¼ tsp cumin

½ cup chopped pumpkin seeds, for garnish

DIRECTIONS:

Using a food processor or blender, process all ingredients until a smooth paste forms. Stir in the ½ cup of chopped pumpkin seeds and serve.

REUBEN WALNUT PAR-TE WITH ALL THE FIXINS

4 SERVINGS — LEVEL I, LG, AI, SB

This pâté is classy and never boring! I like to serve my raw classic reuben with pickled red onions, scallions, cashew swiss cheeze, and Russian dressing all in a coconut crêpe. It's the perfect meal to make for the people who doubt clean eating . . . for real.

INGREDIENTS:

2 cups walnuts, soaked for at least 4 hours
¼ cup olive oil
2 dates, pitted
1 tsp cinnamon
1 tsp mustard seeds
1 tsp black peppercorns
1 tsp ground cloves
1 tsp allspice
½ tsp ground ginger
½ tsp celery seed
2 tsp sea salt
1 tbsp balsamic vinegar
1 celery stalk
Coconut Wrappers (see page 342)
Cashew Swiss Cheeze (see page 355)
Pickled Red Onions (see page 421)
Russian dressing

DIRECTIONS:

Pulse all ingredients in food processor until the texture is slightly chunky and delicious.

To assemble a wrap, lay a coconut wrapper flat and spread with a layer of the pate and a layer of cheeze. Top with pickled onions, drizzle on some Russian dressing, roll coconut wrapper medium-tight, and enjoy. Serve with extra Russian dressing for dipping.

*For a more no fuss-no muss approach, simply assemble the pate, cheeze, onions, and dressing on a bed of your fave greens and call it a day.

RUSSIAN DRESSING

INGREDIENTS:

2 cups Magic-naise
(recipe on page 418)
½ cup Ketchup (recipe on page 419)
¼ cup apple cider vinegar
1 date, pitted
1 tbsp minced onion
½ tsp sea salt
1 tsp black pepper
½ tsp dill

DIRECTIONS:

In a food processor or blender,
blend all ingredients until
smooth and delicious.

CASHEW SWISS CHEEZE

INGREDIENTS:

1 recipe Fakin' Cream Cheeze (page 411)

DIRECTIONS:

Spread the cheese onto a dehydrator
sheet, about ¼" thick. Dehydrate
on 115°F for 5 to 6 hours until firm
but soft. Slice into triangles.

EGGPLANT PARM WITH BOLOGNESE SAUCE AND RICOTTA

4 SERVINGS — LEVEL 1, LG

This is ultimate comfort food turned ultimate clean fuel. This is an amazing option if you're just starting to delve into the magical world of clean eating or if you're entertaining some friends. This recipe is a bit more laborious but once you're done you'll have eggplant parm in a bolognese sauce with baby spinach and almond ricotta crêpe . . . and you'll be very happy. Promise!

INGREDIENTS:

1 eggplant
Apple cider vinegar
Extra virgin olive oil
1 recipe FUNyon batter and coating (see page 374)

DIRECTIONS:

Cut the eggplant into ¼"-thick rounds. Marinate the eggplant in a mix of 1 part apple cider vinegar to 3 parts oil. Use however much vinegar and oil you need to fully coat the eggplant depending on how big it is. Freeze the eggplant and then thaw.

Dip the thawed eggplant slices first into the FUNyon batter and then the coating. Place on a dehydrator sheet and dehydrate at 115°F for 6 hours, until the outside is crisp and the inside is soft. Set aside. IF you are using an oven, set temp to 225 °F for approx 1.5 hours or until thorougly cooked, with a crisp crust. Transfer eggplant slices to a cutting board and add about 3 tbsp. of the ricotta mixture to the end of one side. Roll up from that side, and place them down. Top with a heapin' helping of Bolognese Sauce. Now that's Italian.

BOLOGNESE SAUCE

INGREDIENTS:

2 large tomatoes

¼ cup sun-dried tomatoes, soaked and drained

1 tbsp apple cider vinegar

2 tbsp diced onion

1 garlic clove

½ tsp oregano

½ tsp dried basil OR 2 tbsp fresh basil

½ cup sun-dried tomatoes, soaked, drained, and chopped

½ cup walnuts, ground into crumbs

1 cup Portobello mushrooms, diced

Salt to taste

DIRECTIONS:

Blend all ingredients—except the second set of sun-dried tomatoes, walnuts, and mushrooms—until smooth. Add the sun-dried tomatoes, walnuts, and mushrooms and mix until combined.

RICOTTA

INGREDIENTS:

2 cups raw pine nuts, soaked

2 tbsps lemon juice

2 tbsps nutritional yeast

1 handful of baby spinach (optional)

1 tsp sea salt

DIRECTIONS:

In a food processor, pulse all ingredients until they form a chunky mixture, adding spinach at the end of the processing.

SNAXXX & TREATS

Smaller bites for when you're
feeling peckish.

[SAVORY]

Feelin' Jerky

2 SERVINGS — LEVEL 1, NF, LG

Remember this: cauliflower has high levels of vitamin-like choline, which helps you sleep well, aids in muscle movement, and keeps your memory in check! In this recipe, the cauliflower becomes addictively chewy with a spicy heat from the sriracha. It may seem like overkill, but salting the cauli before and after dehydration is essential in pulling all the flavors together. Pro tip: sprinkle minced parsley on top for a fresh extra touch.

INGREDIENTS:

Head of cauliflower, separated into small and evenly sized florets

¼ cup + 2 tbsp tahini

2 tbsp onion powder

1 tbsp garlic powder

1 tsp cayenne

2 tsp sriracha

1 tbsp apple cider vinegar

1 tsp liquid smoke (optional)

½ tsp smoked paprika

¼ tsp sea salt, plus more for serving

¼ cup water, or more to make the batter smooth and thick

Minced parsley (optional)

DIRECTIONS:

It's very important to cut the cauliflower florets as small and as evenly as possible, that way the pieces get chewy and have the best flavor.

Combine all ingredients, except the cauliflower and optional parsley, to make a smooth batter (the same consistency of beer batter). If needed, you can add more water to achieve the right consistency.

Toss the florets into the batter until they're all coated well. Spread the florets in an even layer on a dehydrator sheet. Sprinkle sea salt evenly across the top. Dehydrate at 115°F for 12 to 24 hours, keeping in mind that the longer you dehydrate, the crunchier it gets. If you don't have a dehydrator, bake the jerky at 350°F for 45 mins - 1 hour making sure to occasionayly flip over.

Once ready, sprinkle extra salt (to taste) and parsley.

Cauliflower will stay fresh for at least 5 days if stored in an airtight container in the refrigerator. If your cauliflower is more dehydrated and completely dry and crunchy, you can store it in a glass jar in a dark, cool place for up to 1 month.

spicy BUFFALO popcorn

2 SERVINGS — LEVEL 1, AI, NF, LG

Cauliflower is kind of genius. It's perfectly delicious on its own, but it's also a sexy canvas for soooo much flavor. In this recipe, they morph into spicy popcorn that's better than any Poppycock around!

INGREDIENTS:

1 head cauliflower
½ to ¾ cup dates, pitted
¼ cup water
¼ cup sun-dried tomatoes
2 tbsp tahini
1 tbsp apple cider vinegar
1 tsp cayenne pepper
2 tsp garlic powder
2 tsp onion powder
¼ tsp turmeric
2 tbsp nutritional yeast

DIRECTIONS:

Cut the cauliflower into small pieces. Try to cut the florets into as even and small chunks as possible, that way your popcorn will be crunchy.

Combine the rest of the ingredients in a food processor and blender and mix until combined. Toss the florets into the spicy sauce until they're all coated well. Place florets on a dehydrator tray and dehydrate at 115°F for 12 to 24 hours, until you achieve your desired crunchiness. If you dont have a dehydrator, place the popcorn on a baking sheet with a thin layer of coconut oil. Bake at 225°F for 3-5 hours or until crunchy. The longer you dehydrate, the crunchier it'll get.

Popcorn will stay fresh for at least 5 days if stored in an airtight container in the refrigerator. If your cauliflower is more dehydrated and completely dry and crunchy, you can store it in a glass jar in a dark, cool place for up to 1 month.

Jalapeño (Dirty) POPS

20 POPPERS — LEVEL I, AI, LG

Did you say jalapeño? Done!

INGREDIENTS:

20 jalapeños
1 recipe Cashew Cheeze (recipe on page 404)
1 cup almonds, ground
2 tbsp garlic powder
2 tbsp onion powder
1 tbsp salt
Pinch of black pepper
¼ tsp cumin
Pinch of cayenne pepper
¼ tsp paprika

DIRECTIONS:

Cut the jalapeños lengthwise, leaving the cap on. Remove the seeds and any of the white pith. Fill with cashew cheeze and set aside. Combine the rest of the ingredients to create the coating. Dip the stuffed jalapeños in the coating and place in the dehydrator at 115°F for 24 hours. If you dont have a dehydrator, place the popcorn on a baking sheet with a thin layer of coconut oil. Bake at 225˚F for 2.5-3.5 hours until soft and buttery. Or if you're hardcore, eat 'em without dehydrating for that extra blow out yer nasal passages kinda feel.

Get BUFFalo Zucchini Chips with Cool RAWnch

BUFFalo
Zucchini Chips

4 SERVINGS — LEVEL I, AI, SB, LG

Just when you thought zuke couldn't get better, I go and make a chip out of it. Feel free to snack your face off. Also, you're welcome. P.S. serve with Cool RAWnch Sauce for optimum snaxxx time pleasure (see opposite page).

INGREDIENTS:

2 zucchini
2 tbsp garlic powder
2 tbsp extra virgin olive oil
1 tsp cumin
½ tsp smoked paprika
¼ tsp chipotle powder
2 tbsp lemon juice
½ tsp turmeric (optional)

DIRECTIONS:

Use a mandoline to slice the zucchini very thinly. The thicker you slice, the longer it takes to dehydrate and the longer it takes for you to eat them. Set the zukes aside.

In a medium bowl, combine the remaining ingredients until a paste forms. Add the sliced zukes to the bowl and mix thoroughly, but gently, until each one is coated. Place coated zucchini in a dehydrator at 115°F and dehydrate until crispy, about 12 hours. If you do not have a dehydrator, bake in an oven at 225°F for approx 2-3 hours or until crisp.

Cool RAWnch Sauce

INGREDIENTS:

1 cup almond mylk
¼ cup apple cider vinegar
1 cup macademia nuts, soaked
3 tbsp lemon juice
¼ cup extra virgin olive oil
3 soaked dates, pitted
1 tsp dill
1 tsp parsley
1 garlic clove
2 tsp onion powder
½ tsp sea salt
Fresh black pepper, to taste
2 tbsp chopped chives, for garnish
¼ cup minced parsley, for garnish
½ tsp minced dill, for garnish

DIRECTIONS:

Combine the almond mylk and apple cider vinegar to make "buttermilk." Let sit for 10 minutes for flavors to develop.

Combine all the other ingredients in a blender/food processor, except for the garnishes, and blend until smooth. Stir in the chives, parsley, and dill and stir to combine.

Funonion Bread

This "bread" is nutty and incredibly tasty. Plenty of nuts and seeds provide you with protein and fiber that regular bread just doesn't have . . . sorry not sorry, basic bread. Eat it as a sandwich or spread hummus on it for a hearty snack.

INGREDIENTS:

3 yellow onions
1 cup raw sunflower
seeds, ground evenly
½ cup pumpkin seeds, ground evenly
1 cup flaxseeds, ground evenly
½ cup raw almonds, ground evenly
1 tbsp miso
¼ cup Bragg Liquid Aminos OR tamari
2 garlic cloves
½ tsp black pepper

DIRECTIONS:

Peel and halve the onions. Slice in a food processor using the slicing disc attachment. Place the sliced onions in a large bowl with the rest of the ingredients until thoroughly combined.

Spread the mixture over a dehydrator sheet and repeat until all the mixture is used (I ended up using 2 sheets). Dehydrate at 115°F for 18 hours, then flip over and continue dehydrating for 6 more hours. If you dont have a dehydrator, spread the mixture on a baking sheet coated with a thin layer of coconut oil. Bake at 225°F for 3-6 hours or until bread is completely dry on both sides.

Cut into 9 equal pieces, then cut in half.

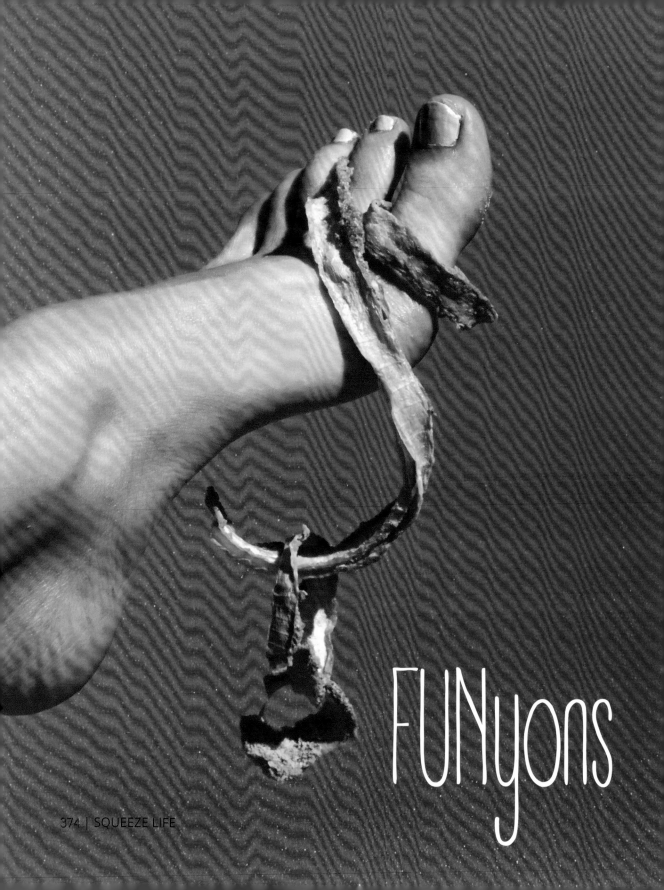

FUNyons

INGREDIENTS:

4 yellow onions, sliced into ½"-thick rings

For the batter:

1 cup buckwheat, soaked

2 tbsp flaxseeds, ground

2 garlic cloves

1½ to 2 cups water

¼ cup extra virgin olive oil

For the coating:

1 cup nutritional yeast

1 cup almonds, ground

1 tbsp garlic powder

1 tbsp sea salt

½ tsp black pepper

¼ tsp cumin

⅛ tsp cayenne pepper

½ tsp paprika

DIRECTIONS:

Blend all batter ingredients until smooth. Set aside.

Toss all coating ingredients together until well mixed. Dip the onion slices into the batter, shaking off any excess, and dip into the coating mixture.

Place on a dehydrator sheet and dehydrate at 115°F for 12 to 16 hours, or until crisp. If you dont have a dehydrator, spread the mixture on a baking sheet coated with a thin layer of coconut oil. Bake at 225°F for 3-6 hours or until crisp.

4 SERVINGS
LEVEL 1, SB, LG

Onions were used for medicinal purposes back in da day, that's how magical they are. Nowadays they're still used for the same wondrous purposes, but now you can eat 'em as goddamn FUNyons and reap all the benefits! Onions are the richest dietary source of a potent antioxidant called quercetin, that's been known to lower cholesterol, raise good cholesterol, fight asthma, and ward off infections.

[BREAKY AND SWEET TREATS]

DID YA KNOW? Apples give ya more energy than a cup of coffee! If you're feeling sleepy, grab an apple and ditch the caffeine.

SUPERcharged Cinnamon Oatmeal

4-6 SERVINGS — LEVEL I, AI

There's nothing like some RAWnchiness in the morning (or in the afternoon . . . or at night . . . or anytime, really). This completely raw oatmeal is packed with fiber, protein, and sweetness in all the right places.

INGREDIENTS:

2 apples, peeled and cored
1 cup walnuts, soaked overnight, ¼ cup reserved
2 cups steel cut oats, soaked
overnight and rinsed well
1½ to 2¼ cups water
2 tbsp chia seeds
1 tbsp cinnamon
1 tsp vanilla
½ tsp sea salt
½ cup soaked dates, pitted
Almonds and/or raisins, soaked (optional)

DIRECTIONS:

Dice the apples but keep the chunks from 1 apple in a separate bowl and set aside for later. Process the rest of the ingredients except the reserved walnuts until creamy but not totally smooth. Mix in the diced apple and remaining walnuts and serve.

Ain't It a PITAYA Bowl

INGREDIENTS:

1 cup dragon fruit, peeled

½ frozen banana

1/3 cup coconut mylk, or whatever mylk you like

½ cup frozen blueberries

½ tbsp coconut butter (optional, for added creaminess)

DIRECTIONS:

Using a food processor or blender, puree all ingredients until silky smooth. Top with whatever toppings your heart desires!

I LIKE TO USE:

Sliced bananas

Granola

Shredded coconut

Goji berries

Mulberries

Blueberries

Raspberries

Blackberries

Flaxseeds

Almond butter

Cacao nibs

2 SERVINGS
LEVEL 1, AI, SB, NF

Açai bowls are soo last year. Thai pitaya bowls are where it's at for a healthy, filling snaxxx and/or breakfast! Pitayas a.k.a. dragon fruit have more antioxidants than the so-called superfood açai, sorry Brazilian babes! This recipe is similar to a smoothie bowl, but way silkier and topped with whatever toppings you have on hand. Easy!

Cinnamon Coconut Yogurt Bowl

4 SERVINGS — LEVEL I, AI, NF

Probiotic literally means the promotion of life in Greek, and that's what this sexy bowl of yogurt will do to ya. Probiotics are known for being incredibly useful in ailing any gastrointestinal probs, and while that's so true, they're even more powaful! They can help to balance your immune system and keep yo urinary health in check. Probiotics are especially great for all you ladies out there with any vag yeast infections since it balances out the levels of bacteria.

INGREDIENTS:

2 cups coconut meat
1½ cups coconut water
2 capsules probiotics (I like Sunbiotics)
1 tsp cinnamon
1 tbsp maple syrup
Seasonal fruit, for serving
Cacao nibs (optional), for serving

DIRECTIONS:

In a blender or food processor, blend the coconut meat and coconut water until smooth and creamy. Add the probiotics and blend some more until incorporated. Add the mixture to a clean container and lid it, or you can cover it with cheesecloth/mesh fabric.

Leave it at room temperature for 12 to 24 hours. The longer it ferments, the freakier and funkier it'll be. So if you like it sour and tangy, leave it out for 24 hours, but if you're more conservative, you can put it in the fridge to stop the fermentation process. Mix in cinnamon and maple syrup.

My fave way of serving this is to pour it over seasonal fruit and add some cacao nibs for a crunch and a JOLT.

I Want Candy

MESQUITE WALNUTS

4 SERVINGS — LEVEL I, AI, SB

Thanks to artificially flavored chips, the world now thinks mesquite means BBQ. Wrong. Mesquite powder is actually made by grinding the pods from the mesquite tree. It doesn't taste at all BBQ-y; instead it's sweet, nutty, and caramel-like. It's a great natural sweetener for desserts, but I like dressing up nuts with it for a sweet snack. If you're not crazy about walnuts, feel free to swap it for something else.

INGREDIENTS:

1/3 cup dates, soaked and pureed
1 tbsp mesquite powder
1 tsp lime juice
½ tsp vanilla
Pinch of sea salt
¼ tsp cinnamon
2 cups walnuts

DIRECTIONS:

Whisk all ingredients, except for the walnuts, until thoroughly combined. Add the walnuts and toss until coated. Spread the mixture onto a nonstick dehydrator sheet, such as Teflex, and dehydrate at 115°F for 12 to 16 hours until the nuts are dry. If you dont have a dehydrator, spread the mixture on a baking sheet coated with a thin layer of coconut oil. Bake at 225°F for 4-5 hours or until nuts are dry.

Spicy (Cashew) Nuts

4 SERVINGS — LEVEL I, AI

Nuts are great, in general and as snaxxx. These nuts are spicy with a hint of sweetness, making them absolutely addictive. You can always swap cashews for a different nut if you're not all that into them.

INGREDIENTS:

4 tbsp coconut nectar OR maple syrup
1½ tsp curry powder
1 tsp Bragg Liquid Aminos
1 tsp lemon juice
¼ tsp sea salt
2 cups cashews

DIRECTIONS:

Whisk all ingredients, except for the cashews, until thoroughly combined. Add the cashews and toss until coated. Spread the mixture onto a nonstick dehydrator sheet, such as Teflex, and dehydrate for 24 hours at 115°F until the nuts are dry. If you dont have a dehydrator, spread the mixture on a baking sheet coated with a thin layer of coconut oil. Bake at 225°F for 4-5 hours. The nuts will be sticky. Don't worry, that's totally cool.

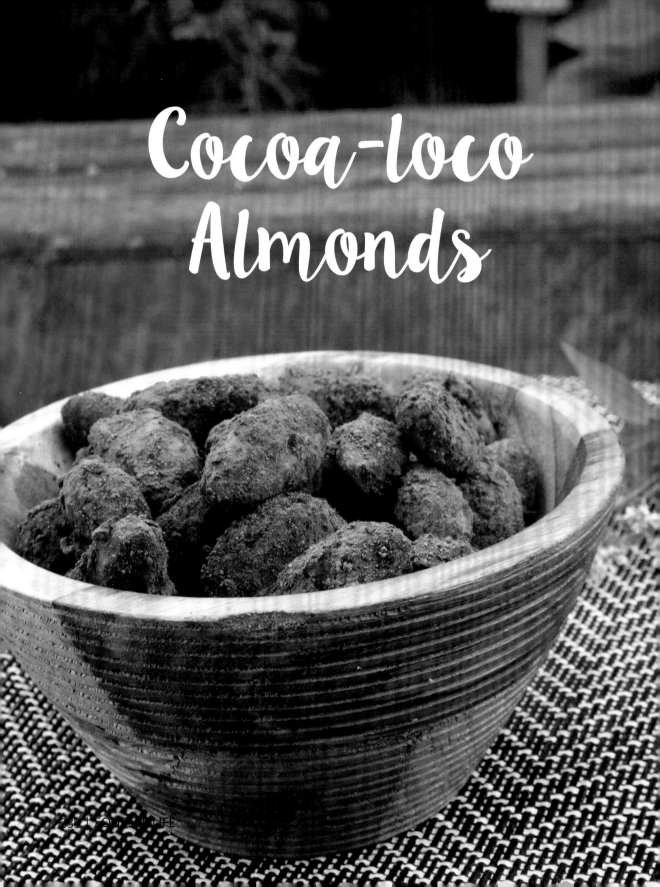

Cocoa-loco
Almonds

5 SERVINGS — LEVEL I, SB, AI

Almonds are the ideal hungry mood snack 'cause they satiate and give you an energy boost. These are dusted with cocoa to satisfy your sweet cravings while keeping you looking sweet!

INGREDIENTS:

¼ cup coconut nectar OR maple syrup
½ tsp vanilla extract
Pinch of sea salt
4 tsp cocoa powder
2 tsp coconut sugar
1 tbsp lacuma
2½ cups almonds

DIRECTIONS:

Whisk all ingredients, except for the almonds, until thoroughly combined. Add the almonds and toss until coated. Spread the mixture onto a nonstick dehydrator sheet, such as Teflex, and dehydrate at 115°F for 12 to 16 hours until the nuts are dry. If you dont have a dehydrator, spread the mixture on a baking sheet coated with a thin layer of coconut oil. Bake at 225°F for 2.5-3 hours or until nuts are dry.

ORANGE blossom BACK-LOVAH

8 SERVINGS — LEVEL I, SB, AI

This protein-packed Middle-Eastern sweet pastry, traditionally made with filo, chopped nuts and honey (AKA baklava) is recreated by yours truly as a healthy treat. The citrus adds a nice balance to the sweetness of the maple syrup so you won't go into a sugah shock, sugar.

INGREDIENTS:

4½ tbsp maple syrup OR coconut nectar
1 tsp lemon juice
1 tsp orange juice
2 tsp orange zest
1 tsp ground cinnamon
½ tsp vanilla extract
Pinch of sea salt
½ tsp ground cloves
1 tsp orange blossom water (optional)
½ cup pecans
½ cup almonds
½ cup pistachios
½ cup pine nuts

DID YA KNOW? Semen is pretty low in calories (anywhere between 5 to 25 calories) and it contains vitamin C. Snaxxx time indeed.

DIRECTIONS:

Whisk all ingredients, except for the nuts, until thoroughly combined. Add the nuts and toss until coated. Spread the mixture onto a non-stick dehydrator sheet, such as Teflex, and dehydrate at 115°F for 24 hours until the nuts are dry. If you dont have a dehydrator, spread the mixture on a baking sheet coated with a thin layer of coconut oil. Bake at 225 °F for 3-4 hours or until nuts are dry.

Hazelnut Butter Cups

8 SERVINGS — LEVEL I, AI

Treat yo' self. TREAT. YO'. SELF. These cups are like treating yourself twice, once 'cause it's so good, and the second because it's so good for your bod. Feel free to swap the hazelnut butter for almond butter if that's what you have on hand.

INGREDIENTS:

Hazelnut Butter Layer:
¼ cup coconut oil
½ cup hazelnut butter
1 tsp almond extract
1 tsp vanilla extract
1 tbsp maple syrup

DIRECTIONS:

Melt the coconut oil over a double boiler on low heat. Add the hazelnut butter, almond extract, vanilla extract, and maple syrup and whisk until it's completely smooth.

Remove the filled cupcake molds from the freezer and pour the hazelnut layer on top of the chocolate, filling the molds about halfway. Place the molds back in the freezer for 15 minutes, then pour the rest of the chocolate mixture. Place molds back in the freezer for at least 1 hour. DEVOUR!

INGREDIENTS:

Chocolate Layer:
1 cup raw cacao butter
1 cup raw cacao powder
PInch of sea salt
1/3 cup maple syrup

DIRECTIONS:

Slice the cacao butter into thin slices. Melt the cacao butter over a double boiler on low heat. Mix the cacao powder and salt in a medium bowl, and add the melted cacao butter to it. Add the maple syrup and mix well to remove any lumps.

Pour the chocolate mixture into cupcake molds, only filling up 1/3 of the way. Make sure to only use ½ of the chocolate mixture (you'll need the other half later). Place molds in the freezer to set while you make the hazelnut layer.

Maple Crème Brûlée

4 SERVINGS — LEVEL I, AI, SB

This is one of my favorite treats ever. It's incredibly rich, creamy, and completely dairy-free. Please use some good quality maple syrup, it really makes a difference!

INGREDIENTS:

1½ cups cashews
½ cup maple syrup
½ cup pine nuts
⅔ cup coconut butter
1 tsp lemon juice
Pinch of sea salt
1½ tsp chia seeds, ground
2 vanilla beans, scraped OR
1 tsp vanilla extract
Maple syrup, for serving

DIRECTIONS:

Blend cashews and maple syrup until smooth. Add the rest of the ingredients and continue blending until completely silky. Add the mixture into ramekins and freeze for 30 minutes, then transfer to the fridge until firm.

When ready to serve, turn over onto a plate and drizzle with some extra maple syrup. Oh yeah, *you fancy.*

Apricot-Lavender Fruit Leather

INGREDIENTS:

5 cups chopped apricot

3 tbsp maple syrup

½ tsp lavender, ground

DIRECTIONS:

In a blender or food processor, puree all ingredients until smooth. Taste and adjust according to taste, sweetening some more if needed. Keep in mind that the flavors will intensify as they dehydrate. If you sweetened more, make sure to give it a good pulse so everything's well incorporated.

Lightly coat the dehydrator sheet with coconut oil spray to prevent sticking. The fruit roll up will expand as it dehydrates so make sure to give it some room for expansion. Spread it as evenly as possible.

Dehydrate at 115°F for 12 to 15 hours, until it is pliable and easy to roll. If there are dark spots that means the fruit leather is not completely dry. Under-dried leather will mold and over-dried leather will become hard and crispy.

Wrap in plastic and store in the fridge for up to 3 days.

6 SERVINGS – LEVEL 1, SB, NF, AI

Chill out with this old school snack. Literally. Lavender is known for its soothing and calming properties, so munch on this leather if you're feeling stressed or anxious (or hungry). Apricots are great sources of fiber and antioxidants that protect you from free-radicals, enhance your eyesight, and are anti-inflammatory.

Raspberry-Chia Fruit Roll Up

4 SERVINGS — LEVEL 1, AI, NF, SB

Chia seeds have an amazing amount of protein, healthy fats (omega-3s), and dietary fiber. They're also ideal for thickening up smoothies, puddings, and any creamy recipe.

INGREDIENTS:

4 cups fresh raspberries

2 tbsp chia seeds, ground

1 tsp ground cinnamon

1 tbsp maple syrup OR coconut nectar

1 tsp fresh lemon juice

1 tbsp vanilla extract

½ cup of gelled Irish moss

DIRECTIONS:

In a blender or food processor, combine all ingredients and process until completely smooth. Allow the chia to thicken the puree for about 10 minutes. Spray a dehydrator Teflex sheet with coconut oil spray and distribute the mixture evenly on it. Dehydrate at 115°F for 13 to 15 hours, flipping halfway.

Wrap in plastic wrap and store in the fridge for up to 3 days.

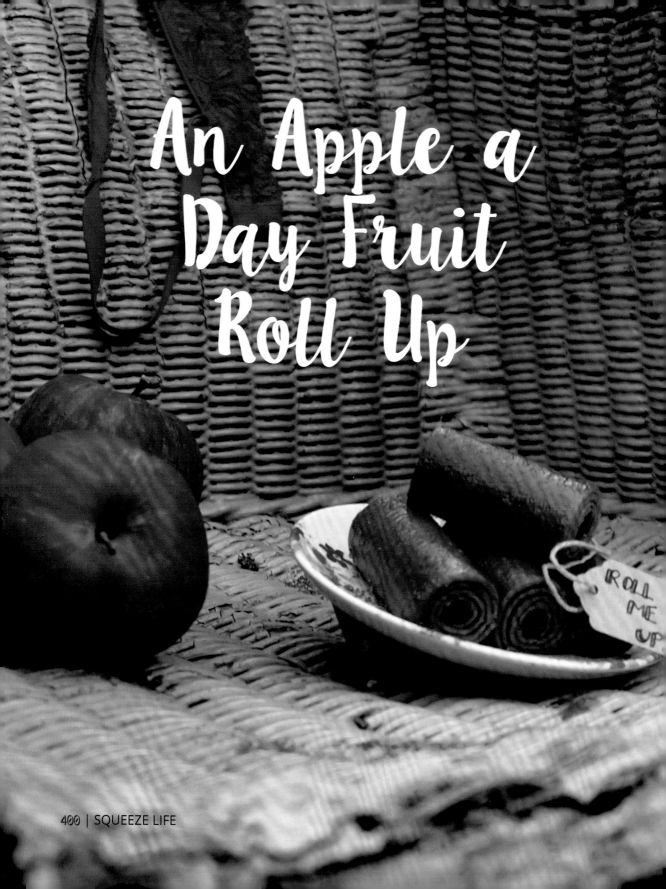

An Apple a Day Fruit Roll Up

6 SERVINGS — LEVEL 1, AI, NF, SB

It really does keep the doctor away. It has antioxidants which aid in cell regeneration, it regulates blood sugar, which prevents diabetes, and it even cleans your teeth (the chewing you do when you eat an apple causes saliva to form in the mouth, and that saliva keeps bacteria at bay).

INGREDIENTS:

3 green apples, cored and seeded
2 large bananas, peeled
2 tbsp coconut sugar
1 tsp cinnamon
⅛ tsp sea salt
⅛ tbsp chia seeds, ground

DIRECTIONS:

In a blender or food processor, combine all ingredients and process until it's completely smooth. Allow the chia to thicken the puree for about 10 minutes. Spray a dehydrator Teflex sheet with coconut oil spray and distribute the mix evenly on it. Dehydrate at 115°F for 13 to 15 hours, flipping halfway.

Wrap in plastic wrap and store in the fridge for up to 3 days.

[SPREADS & CONDOM-ENTS]

Spread 'em! Slather these wherever
your heart desires (*wink, wink*)
and feel good about it.

FETA CHEEZE

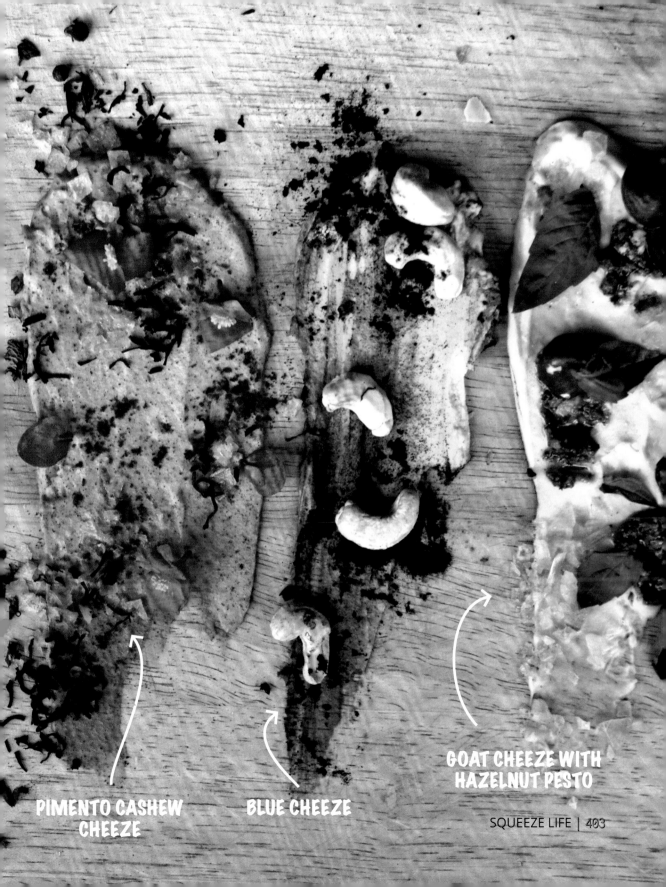

PIMENTO CASHEW
CHEEZE

BLUE CHEEZE

GOAT CHEEZE WITH
HAZELNUT PESTO

Cashew Cheeze

YIELDS 2½ CUPS — LEVEL I, LG

Cheesy like cheese, but hearty and protein-packed like cashews. Confusing and delicious.

INGREDIENTS:

2 cups cashews, soaked

1½ tsp sea salt

¼ tsp white pepper

1 tsp probiotics (I like Sunwarrior)

1 tsp onion powder

1 tsp miso (optional, for added umami-ness)

Water, for blending

DIRECTIONS:

Using a blender or food processor, blend all ingredients until smooth. Use however much water you need to blend everything into a cohesive paste. Place inside a container and lightly cover it with a lid or cheesecloth. Allow to sit at room temperature overnight.

The key factors of the fermentation process are the strength of your probiotics and the temperature of your kitchen. If it's cold, the fermentation will be slower and vice versa.

For a tangier cheese, leave your cheeze out at room temperature for anytime between 12 hours to 5 days. Whenever you're happy with the taste, put it in the fridge to stop fermentation.

NOTE:

If you don't have time to ferment, simply replace the probiotics with tablespoons of lemon juice.

Hemp Cheeze

YIELDS 2½ CUPS
LEVEL 1, LG, AI, SB

Hemp seeds are a superfood, so this is officially super cheeze. The macadamia nuts add an extra creamy silkiness and healthy fatty oils.

INGREDIENTS:

1 cup hemp seeds

1 cup macadamia nuts

2 garlic cloves

1½ tsp sea salt

¼ tsp black pepper

1 tsp probiotics (I like Sunwarrior)

1 tsp miso (optional, for added umami-ness)

Water, for blending

DIRECTIONS:

Using a blender or food processor, blend all ingredients until smooth. Use however much water you need to blend everything into a cohesive paste. Place inside a container and lightly cover it with a lid or cheesecloth. Allow to sit at room temperature overnight.

The key factors of the fermentation process are the strength of your probiotics and the temperature of your kitchen. If it's cold, the fermentation will be slower and vice versa.

For a tangier cheese, leave your cheeze out at room temperature for anytime between 12 hours to 5 days. Whenever you're happy with the taste, put it in the fridge to stop fermentation.

Seed Cheeze

YIELDS 2½ CUPS
LEVEL 1, LG, SB, NF

Who knew you could make cheeze out of SEEDS? What a wonderful world we live in.

INGREDIENTS:

1 cup sunflower seeds, soaked
1 cup pumpkin seeds, soaked
1½ tsp sea salt
Water, for blending
¼ tsp black pepper
1 tsp probiotics (I like Sunwarrior)
1 tsp miso (optional, for added umami-ness)

DIRECTIONS:

Using a blender or food processor, blend all ingredients until smooth. Use however much water you need to blend everything into a cohesive paste. Place inside a container and lightly cover it with a lid or cheesecloth. Allow to sit at room temperature overnight.

The key factors of the fermentation process are the strength of your probiotics and the temperature of your kitchen. If it's cold, the fermentation will be slower and vice versa.

For a tangier taste, leave your cheeze out at room temperature for anytime between 12 hours to 5 days. Whenever you're happy with the taste, put it in the fridge to stop fermentation.

JALAPEÑO CREAM CHEEZE

YIELDS 2 CUPS — LEVEL 1, LG

A spiced version of our regular cashew cream cheeze.

INGREDIENTS:

10 small jalapeños , washed, seeded, and ribbed
1 quart Cashew Cheeze (page 404)

DIRECTIONS:

Finely mince your jalapeños and combine with cheeze. Mix well.

DID YA KNOW? A fun way to dress up yo cheeze is to make a cheeze log with herbs and spices. Simply add your base cheeze to a plastic wrap-lined springform pan or round mold, sprinkle on some peppercorns, herbs (whatever kind you like, or even a combo), and salt. Press all the toppings onto the cheese and refrigerate until set. Once you're ready to eat, simply flip the pan over and devour.

FETA CHEEZE

YIELDS 2½ CUPS LG

Nutritional yeast adds an amazing cheezy flavor to whatever you use it in, but combined with lemon it transforms your fave cheeze into straight up feta magic!

INGREDIENTS:

1 Cheeze recipe, whatever your fave is
1 tbsp lemon juice
1 tbsp nutritional yeast

DIRECTIONS:

Combine all ingredients until well mixed. Spread mixture onto a dehydrator sheet about ¼" thick and dehydrate at 115°F for 12 hours, until you reach a drier consistency. If you dont have a dehydrator, spread a thin layer of the cheese on parchment paper, place on a baking sheet and bake at 225°F the cheese at 225°F for 1-2 hours or until al crisp consistency is reached.

DID YA KNOW? Making blue cheeze is easy! Take some cheeze of your choice and freeze it for 1 hour. Take some cashew cheeze (see page 404) and mix it with a bit of spirulina and freeze it for 1 hour. Remove both cheezes from the freezer. They should have a moldable consistency. With your fingers, roughly combine the spirulina cheeze with the white cheeze. Mix until you've reached a desired consistency with big chunks of blue-green goodness. Place in the freezer for 1 hour until the mixture hardens. EAT AWAY!

There's no bacon, cream, or cheese in this recipe but it still tastes heavenly. Snack on veggies dipped in this or slather it on your fave raw breads/crackers.

INGREDIENTS:

1 quart Cashew Cheeze (page 404)

2 tbsp paprika

1 tbsp mustard

1 ½ tsp chipotle powder

1 ½ tsp sea salt

2 ½ tbsp Bragg Liquid Aminos

1 tbsp water

1 tbsp extra virgin olive oil

1 ½ tbsp garlic, finely minced

⅓ tbsp raw mesquite powder

1 bunch of scallions, thinly sliced

DIRECTIONS:

Combine all ingredients together until completely mixed.

FAKIN' CREAM CHEEZE

pimento CASHEW cheeze

YIELDS 3 CUPS — LEVEL I, LG, SB

Pimento cheese is the caviar of the South, and this vegan, healthy version is the caviar of my life.

INGREDIENTS:

½ cup red bell pepper
2 cups raw cashews
½ cup oil
2 garlic cloves
1 tbsp chopped onion
1 tbsp miso
1 tbsp lemon juice
1 tsp probiotics

DIRECTIONS:

Using a food processor or blender, puree all ingredients until smooth. Allow to sit, covered, at room temperature for 24 to 72 hours before serving/devouring.

Vegan Goat Cheeze & Hazelnut Pesto

2½ CUPS — LEVEL I, SB, LG

This pesto is fancy as hell. It's cheesy and hearty thanks to the pesto. I love snacking on this with cruditès, and you will too.

INGREDIENTS:
For the Pesto:
2 cups packed basil
1 garlic clove
½ cup raw hazelnuts
1 tsp miso
6 tbsp extra virgin olive oil
Sea salt and pepper, to taste

DIRECTIONS:

Using a food processor or blender, puree all ingredients until silky smooth. Adjust salt and pepper according to taste.

Swirl the goat cheeze and pesto together and serve.

INGREDIENTS:
For the Vegan Goat Cheese:
½ cup cheeze, whatever your fave is
½ lime, juiced
1 tsp apple cider vinegar
½ tsp salt

DIRECTIONS:

Using a food processor or blender, puree all ingredients until silky smooth.

SUN-DRIED TOMATO &
RED PEPPER
(NO BEAN) HUMMUS

YIELDS 3 CUPS
LEVEL 1, SB, NF, AI, LG

This tomato-y take on the regular hummus is amaaaaazing with crudités, on sandies, wraps or just on top of salads for some extra protein.

INGREDIENTS:

1 medium zucchini, peeled and chopped

1 red bell pepper, seeded and chopped

¾ cups sun-dried tomatoes

1 to 1½ tbsp finely chopped garlic, depending on how garlicky you like your hummus

½ cup raw tahini

¼ cup fresh lemon juice

1 tbsp cold-pressed extra virgin olive oil

½ tsp Celtic sea salt

¾ tsp paprika (optional)

⅛ tsp cayenne pepper (optional)

DIRECTIONS:

Using a food processor or blender, puree all ingredients until smooth and creamy.

YIELDS 3 CUPS — LEVEL I, LG, AI

Tastes like the real deal because it's actually better than the real deal.

INGREDIENTS:

½ tsp mustard powder

⅛ tsp turmeric

¼ tsp sea salt

½ garlic clove

¼ tsp black pepper

¼ cup raw cashews

½ cup water

2 tbsp apple cider vinegar

2 cups avocado OR flaxseed oil

DIRECTIONS:

Using a food processor or blender, puree all ingredients until silky smooth.

MAGIC-NAISE

Ketchup

The condiment game is pretty important, and this raw 'chup is life-changing. Use it as you would the traditional fare, but knowing that this won't permanently take camp in your body (gross).

INGREDIENTS:

1 cup diced tomatoes
3 tbsp dates
¼ cup olive oil
1 tbsp apple cider vinegar
½ tsp onion powder
½ cup sun-dried tomatoes, soaked and drained

DIRECTIONS:

Using a food processor or blender, puree all ingredients until smooth and ketchup-y. Ta-da!

Garden Pâté

YIELDS 3 CUPS — LEVEL I, SB, LG, AI

This pâté is fresh and colorful, the perfect summertime dip!

INGREDIENTS:

½ tsp salt
1 cup raw almonds, soaked
½ cup pecans
1 tbsp fresh ginger
1 garlic clove
1 carrot
2 celery stalks, chopped
1 spring onion, sliced
1½ tbsp olive oil
2 tbsp lemon juice
¼ bunch of fresh basil
¼ bunch of fresh parsley

DIRECTIONS:

Using a food processor or blender, pulse all ingredients until well combined but still slightly chunky.

DID YA KNOW? It's so hard to kick your cheese habit because cheese is filled with protein fragments that have an opioid effect. YUP! Cheese produces euphoric feelings similar to the ones from opium. Now that's milky business!

PICKLED RED ONIONS

These are the best condiments on just about anything. They're great for salads, raw sandwiches, and just for adding a nice tang to any meal. Not to mention that onions are extremely anti-inflammatory and improve overall circulation.

INGREDIENTS:

1 red onion, sliced into thin rounds
3 cups water, boiling
¼ cup apple cider vinegar
1 tbsp pink peppercorns
1 bay leaf
1 garlic clove, smashed
A few pinches of salt

DIRECTIONS:

Place your onions into a sieve over the sink and pour the boiling water over them. Drain and add the onions to a shallow bowl. Add the apple cider vinegar and all other ingredients to the bowl, stir, and let sit on the counter for about 30 minutes. Store, in an airtight container in the fridge, for up to 3 weeks.

RESOURCES

Blue Mountain Organics (www.bluemountainorganics.com):
seeds, nuts, beans, grains, flours, protein powders.

Sunfood Superfoods (www.sunfood.com): acai powder, agave nectar, cacao, coconut oil, goji berries, maca, protein powders, chlorella, spirulina, nuts, and seeds.

Ultimate Superfoods (www.ultimatesuperfoods.com): nuts and seeds, dried fruits, cacao, turmeric, maca, coconut oil, chlorella, spirulina.

Nuts Online (www.nuts.com): nuts, dried fruits, raw cacao nibs, seeds, spirulina.

NuNaturals, Inc. (www.nunaturals.com): stevia, coconut sugar, supplements.

Nutiva (www.nutiva.com): coconut oil, hemp seeds, chia seeds, coconut sugar.

Artisana Organics (www.artisanaorganics.com): nut and seed butters and coconut oil.

Living Harvest (www.livingharvest.com): go-to for your hemp needs.

Sunwarrior (www.sunwarrior.com): all-natural protein powders and supplements.

Garden of Life (www.gardenoflife.com): all-natural proteins and supplements.

Vega (www.myvega.com): plant-based meal replacements.

Pure joy Planet (www.purejoyplanet.com): nut milk bags.

Paderno (www.paderno.com): spiralizers.

Vitamix (www.vitamix.com): high-performance blenders.

Excalibur (www.excaliburdehydrator.com): food dehydrator.

Cuisinart (www.cuisinart.com): food processors.

High Vibe (www.highvibe.com): Waterwizard Counter-top Water Filter.

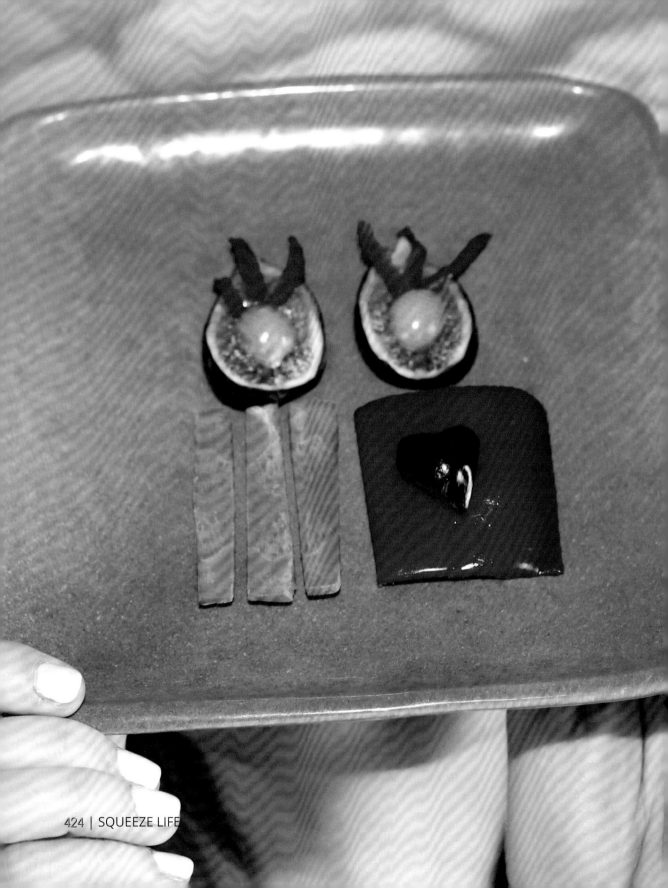

ABOUT THE AUTHOR

Karliin Brooks is the author of this book (duh) and the founder of The Squeeze, a cleansing and juicing lifestyle brand located in New York City. She's an eco warrior, juice queen, and lover of all things. Upon learning about the food industry during her high school years, Karliin immediately turned to a cruelty-free vegan diet and hasn't looked back since. She attended NYU, where she graduated with degrees for Broadcast Journalism and Nutrition, and she received her culinary training at the Natural Gourmet Institute. Karliin is also a former model, freelance producer, and owner of a movie location company in NYC. She left her career in TV production to pursue a life dedicated to changing hearts, minds, and tummies. She's ready to veg-ucate the world.

She turned to a juicing and cleansing lifestyle when she was diagnosed with Grave's disease. Rather than looking forward to a life filled with health complications, Karliin embraced detoxing instead. Not only did she notice physical improvements almost immediately, but her spiritual state improved immensely. Her lack of health led her to a life dedicated to continuously improving herself and others around her. Karliin lives in NYC in an animal rescue shelter, a.k.a. her lovely apartment. She's expanding The Squeeze until it takes over the world and everyone drinks a green juice instead of coffee in the morning. She wants YOU to be healthy, happy, and at peace.

GRATITUDE

I feel tremendously blessed to be surrounded by such a talented, powerful, brilliant, and trailblazing team of visionary go-getters. It is with humble gratitude that I acknowledge the impact of the following individuals who wholeheartedly contributed their energy to "project juice":

First and foremost, I would like to thank my mum for standing beside me through my life. In fact, my whole life. Her unwavering support and unquestioning belief in me has been my inspiration and motivation for continuing to improve, overcome challenges, and remain true to myself and to follow my personal legend of veg-ucating the world.

To my dad who always believed I could do anything I put my mind to. He is my rock and I dedicate this book to him.

An enormous thank you to my sister, Sydra, for bringing energy, love, support and an incredible attention to detail on this book. Just when I thought I couldn't get any more neurotic!

. . . I also want to thank my three rescues: Jabba, Marvin, and Emily for keeping me company and keeping me entertained during countless hours of r+f and writing. Adopt a rescue animal if you can!

Layla, there aren't many professional photographers who will work around the clock on a loco timeline like you did, phoning it in from Hawaii, no less! Thank you for taking thousands of photographs in pursuit of getting that perfect shot. And thank you for making photo editing so seamless.

A huge thank you to Vienna for using your gifted artistic sensibilities to create a flawless design for this book with the help of Peter and Abigail. Thank you design team for generating and capturing such boundless energy and passion. Even in the darkest hours, and there were too many to count on all of our hands and feet, you found a graceful solution. Abigail, you have been a consistent source of confidence, relieve and encouragement though-out this very harried project.

Marko, I will always be in debt to you for your endless well of support and brilliance.

An avalanche of gratitude to my dream team: Katherine, Thelma, Nicole, Rebecca, Paul Wharton, Pia, and Frenchie for bringing this entire journey to fruition, and herding this project every step of the way.

Bill , thank you for your smarts, your sense of humor and your inconceivable care for The Squeeze. Paul, you havent been part of The Squeeze team for very long, but you have become damn close to being our most outstanding secret weapon.

Infinite and resounding thanks to Rosemary and Roy for being a part of this journey, and giving such love and attention to what matters most!

Tonya, a well of gratitude for providing the Squeeze book with a stunning backdrop at The Mercedes Club, and for your support and dedication to the brand and to our friendship.

Thank you to the Skyhorse Publishing team for making my vision of this book come to fruition.

INDEX

T